PEER HELPERS PLUS

**A comprehensive training
manual to help student tutors
and other facilitators
make the grade**

Cheryl Brackenbury

Pembroke Publishers Limited

© 1995 Pembroke Publishers Limited
538 Hood Road
Markham, Ontario
L3R 3K9

Canadian Cataloguing in Publication Data

Brackenbury, Cheryl
    Peer helpers plus

ISBN 1-55138-050-1
1. Peer-group tutoring of students.
2. Group work in education.
3. Peer counseling
I. Title
LB1031.5.B73 1995   371.3'94   c95-930320-0

Editor: Joanne Close

Design & Illustration: Loris Lesynski, MPD & Associates

This book was produced with the generous assistance of the government of Ontario through the Ministry of Culture, Tourism and Recreation.

Printed and bound in Canada by Webcom

9 8 7 6 5 4 3 2 1

Dedication

To my family, especially George, for constant support and encouragement.

To my father, Eric Bradley, who inspires dedication and determination.

To my friend and peer helper mentor, Sid Allcorn.

To all Cobourg East peer helpers, both past and present.

Acknowledgments

Every effort has been made to secure permission for copyright material used in this book, and to acknowledge all sources accordingly. Any errors or omissions brought to our attention will be corrected in future printings.

"A Mathematical Friend": courtesy of Rebecca Tombrook and Kathy Kenyon. "Dear J" letters: courtesy of Jenny Goldring. "I See a Child": courtesy of Cindy Herbert. Poor and active listening techniques lists: courtesy of Caroline McNamara. Overview of facilitative responses: courtesy of Myrick, R.D. & Erney. T. (1978, 1984). *Caring and sharing: Becoming a peer facilitator.* Minneapolis, MN: Educational Media Corporation and Myrick, R.D. & Erney, T. (1979, 1985). *Youth helping youth: A handbook for training peer facilitators.* Minneapolis, MN: Educational Media Corporation. Barriers to effective communication: Accelerated Development, 1994, used with permission and Carr, R. & Saunders, G. (1979). *Peer Counselling Starter Kit.* Victoria, BC: Peer Resources. Clarifying and summarizing scenarios: courtesy of Jay Clayton-Ross. "The Squid": courtesy of Sid Allcorn. Five-step decision making model: courtesy of Myrick R.D. & Erney, T. (1978, 1984). *Caring and sharing: Becoming a peer facilitator.* Minneapolis, MN: Educational Media Corporation.

Table of Contents

continued

Preface

"Are you having trouble finding your class? Let me help you."

"You're feeling upset because you failed a math test. Maybe I can help you with some homework questions and go over that new lesson with you."

"I can understand how you feel about getting cut from the basketball team. I also got cut in my first year, but with practice I made the team the next year. Would you like to play pick-up basketball with us at lunch? We sure could use another player."

"Your father doesn't have a right to hit you like that. I'll go with you to talk to the guidance counsellor."

"You look like you're nervous about giving that speech. Do you want to practise in front of me? I can give you some tips my peer helping advisor gave us in our training sessions for talking in front of people."

"It's okay to cry. I was so sorry to hear that your grandmother died. You must be very sad."

"The computer in the guidance office has a great program that helps you find out about a number of careers. Would you like me to show you how to use it?"

From reading these extracts of peer helpers' conversations, you will probably have a good idea of what constitutes a peer helping program – listening, supporting, trusting, facilitating, referring, helping, sorting out, prioritizing, and caring.

Simply stated, the peer helping program is a professionally organized extension of what happens in schools every day – young people constantly turn to one another for help and support. Peer helping ultimately improves and expands the quantity and quality of available assistance. Teachers and students alike find that the tone or climate of a school becomes more positive when peer helping is offered. Peer helping groups offer a ready-made and accessible group of caring persons who are willing to take on responsibilities within the school and the community as the need arises.

Peer helping is one of the fastest growing student-centered movements today. The reasons for this are many. Young people have tremendous energy and enthusiasm. They have imagination and creative ideas. They genuinely care about others, particularly their friends. They have concerns about the future and how they will find their place in an increasingly competitive world. Peer helping capitalizes on the attributes of students today, as well as on their understanding of what fellow students are thinking and experiencing to offer another source of support.

I am a true believer in the positive power of peers and what peer support can do to:
- turn a negative behavior into a positive behavior,
- help a person get through a difficult time,
- encourage a lonely, depressed person to persevere,
- bolster self-esteem,
- build self-confidence, and
- learn a physical, mental or social skill.

My belief in this power has developed over the years through experience gained from being a camp counsellor, teacher, coach, guidance counsellor, crisis phone-line worker, mentor, and parent.

The positive experiences I have had working with so many caring, enthusiastic people, especially adolescents, have been enjoyable and inspirational… so much so that they make me want to continue working with peer helpers year after year.

I am grateful to have had the opportunity to initiate and co-ordinate the peer helping program at Cobourg East Collegiate. I truly appreciate the support and encouragement of my peers – at Cobourg East, particularly Doug Smith and Marty Halloran; at the Ontario Peer Helpers' Association; and at the National Peer Helpers' Association.

It has been more than a decade since I began my first peer helping program. I look forward to the next decade – training new recruits, redefining goals with veteran peer helpers, meeting new people, and exchanging ideas. It is inspiring to think about peer helping programs – their people, purposes, and power. If you haven't ridden the peer support wave, jump aboard – it's invigorating!

1
Flexible and Beneficial: Peer Helping Programs

Listed here are the numerous benefits that stem from a peer helping program, in the school and the community at large.

Benefits of Peer Helping Programs

For Teachers/Guidance Counsellors/Administrators

- help lighten the load of guidance counsellors, allowing them more time to devote to serious student problems and the provision of more services to the entire student body,
- improve student morale and, subsequently, school morale,
- help with other administrative-based programs such as stay-in-school initiatives and tutoring,
- provide a positive link between the school population and the administration.

For Members of the Student Population

- experience increased opportunities to access a friendly ear,
- have visible positive role models in their school,
- have the opportunity to choose a peer helper that they feel most comfortable with,
- have increased opportunity for additional academic help in the form of tutoring,
- have the chance to explore career opportunities with the assistance of a peer helper.

For Peer Helpers

- develop confidence in their own abilities,
- experience a feeling of contribution,
- enhance self-esteem,
- learn problem-solving and decision-making skills,
- develop assertiveness,
- learn and practise good communication skills,
- learn active listening techniques,
- learn time-management skills,
- learn and practise empathetic responses to a range of feelings.

For the Community

- agencies and centers such as senior citizens' homes, food banks, crisis phone lines, and health organizations benefit from volunteer work,
- area schools and students can receive valuable assistance from trained peer helpers, especially in the transition area.

Who Should Use 'Peer Helpers Plus'?

This book is aimed at training students in a high school setting, but can be effectively adapted for use by all peer support groups, for example, facilitators for crisis phone lines and eating disorder clinics.

This leadership training program can be used for any age group from about Grade 6 through high school to college and university. It can be used in a volunteer or credit program to train students in any type of leadership role, whether the program be known as peer tutors, mentors, ambassadors, helpers, or facilitators. Some ways it may be used include:

- by homeroom and/or subject teachers to help students get to know one another, and improve listening, communication, decision-making and problem-solving skills. Learning about and practising all of these skills will, in turn, help with class discussions, small-group work, presentations, and conflict management.
- by guidance counsellors to train peer helpers in ethics, confidentiality, tutoring skills, self-esteem enhancers, group dynamics, friendliness, assertiveness, effective communication, listening, decision-making and problem-solving skills, and educational and career awareness.
- by student council advisors to facilitate leadership training with the student executive and homeroom representatives.
- by school administrators to facilitate workshops with staff regarding effective listening and communication skills, empathy, school-community projects, and fundraising. An appreciation and awareness of students' needs, fears, and hopes may also be addressed and heightened when reading case studies and completing exercises.

Aspects of this book can be used in the following content areas:
- in Guidance for peer helping courses, both volunteer and credit, peer tutoring, mentoring, mediation (conflict resolution), career and educational awareness groups or classes, and support groups (e.g., bereavement, living on one's own, assertiveness, building self-esteem).

- in Physical and Health Education for leadership courses and coaching theory, mental health, communication and perception, building self-esteem and assertiveness, and decision-making and problem-solving segments of the curriculum.
- in Special Education to teach self-esteem, assertiveness, values clarification, decision making, problem solving, and educational awareness.
- in Business Education to teach time-management skills, self-esteem, assertiveness, and decision-making and problem-solving skills.
- in Co-operative Education for reflective learning segments that teach communication and listening skills for job interviews and good employer-employee working relations. Decision-making, problem-solving, values clarification, educational awareness, self-esteem, and assertiveness sections can also be tapped to reinforce various aspects of in-school teaching segments.
- in Life Skills, Personal Life Management, and Career Planning courses to teach self-awareness and build self-esteem, assertiveness, decision-making, problem-solving, values clarification, communication, and listening skills, and educational awareness.
- in Family Studies and Society courses to teach problem-solving, self-esteem, decision-making, and self-awareness skills.
- in Adult Education and Retraining courses to build self-esteem, assertiveness, communication and listening skills, decision-making and problem-solving techniques. The educational awareness and research section will also be of great value.
- in all core subject areas – English, Mathematics, Science, Languages, History, Geography, and Technology – to reinforce good communication and listening skills, and decision-making and problem-solving skills. For students who wish to tutor in one or more areas, work on awareness of feelings, values clarification, confidentiality, trust, ethics and communication, listening, and decision-making skills will all come into play.

A Cross-Curricular Matrix

Subject

Skill

Skill	Guidance	Business Education	Adult Education	Special Education	Co-operative Education	Physical & Health Education	Family Studies	Personal Life Mgt. (Life Skills)	Technology	English	Math & science, History	Language & Geography
Decision Making	✓	✓	✓	✓	✓	✓	✓	✓	✓	✓	✓	✓
Problem Solving	✓	✓	✓	✓	✓	✓	✓	✓	✓	✓	✓	✓
Assertiveness	✓	✓	✓	✓	✓	✓	✓	✓	✓			
Self-Esteem Enhancers	✓			✓	✓		✓	✓				
Confidentiality, Trust, Ethics	✓	✓	✓	✓	✓			✓		✓	✓	✓
Values Clarification	✓		✓	✓	✓	✓	✓	✓	✓	✓	✓	✓
Awareness of Feelings	✓	✓	✓	✓		✓		✓		✓	✓	✓
Active Listening	✓	✓	✓	✓	✓		✓	✓	✓	✓	✓	✓
Communication Skills	✓	✓	✓	✓	✓	✓	✓	✓	✓	✓	✓	✓
Educational & Career Awareness	✓	✓	✓	✓	✓	✓	✓	✓	✓	✓	✓	✓

2
Establishing a Peer Helper Program

Peer Helper Program Requirements

Each school is different in size, number of students and teachers, ethnicity, percentage of basic-, general-, and advanced-level students, locale, and special needs programs.

Like each school, each peer helping program is unique and specific to the school's and students' needs, the advisor's interests and capabilities, and the personality of that particular group of peer helpers.

If you are the advisor for the program, you will probably be responsible for the training of the peer helpers, the maintenance of the program and, in turn, the credibility of the entire peer helping program. The program will go in the direction you wish to lead it. It's a big responsibility and one that has to be planned for carefully. In the Appendix on page 88 is an Advisor's Checklist comprising questions you should consider before training peer helpers – questions that you can ask yourself, your colleagues, and the administration before beginning to initiate any aspect of a peer helping program.

When you have completed the checklist and are certain of the type of program you wish to initiate, you will need to seek the support of the following sectors of the school community:
- administrators,
- staff, students, and parents,
- enthusiastic advisors who can make a substantial time commitment and have training in counselling skills,
- minimal financial commitment, depending on your group's goals and roles.

The first step, of course, is to approach your school principal and/or vice-principal. Without support from this quarter, your group will not exist. If they greet your idea with a positive reaction, speak with a few teachers whom you believe might be interested in helping to create and maintain such a program. Peer helping programs, while of great benefit to the students and the school as a whole, are labor-intensive projects that require time and commitment from staff dedicated to its success.

If you have the support of several staff members and the vice-principal and/or principal, you might want to approach those students whom you believe to be potential peer helpers. While a more in-depth analysis of personality traits of peer helpers is given in the next column, you are, in essence, searching for mature students who are capable of handling their course work, as well as any additional work that arises from their involvement with the peer helping program.

Finally, ask for permission to outline the peer helping program at the next regular staff meeting. While most members will have a general idea of what makes up a peer helping program, you can outline specifics of what you believe the program could do for the school, and where the program's emphasis may lie, for example, in a largely tutorial role or a more generalized helper role. Input from supportive staff and administrators can help you tailor the program's goals to most closely reflect the school's needs.

Qualities to Look for in Potential Peer Helpers

Peer helpers must be chosen carefully since the program is only as effective as the individuals involved. There are a number of qualities that most students should have in order to be considered as potential peer helpers. Look for students who:
- demonstrate emotional maturity,
- exhibit reasonable and reliable behavior,
- display leadership ability,
- relate well to others,
- have a warm, friendly personality,
- have a positive attitude,
- have a concern for others, and wish to help them,
- have respect for the feelings of others and for their privacy,
- are good role models for their peers,
- are successful academically,
- have a good attendance record.

Starting Considerations

1. In your first year, keep the group small, perhaps six to eight students.
2. Try to encourage male students to become involved. Chances are that most of your applicants will be female.
3. Select students in their middle high school years. First-year students are caught up in adjusting to high school. Senior students are primarily concentrating on obtaining high marks in their courses. If, however, senior students have a study period, they may want to offer their services, especially if

they have been a peer helper before.

4. Be cautious of the student already heavily involved in school and/or community activities. Peer helping requires a good deal of time, both for training and for the ensuing activities the group takes on.

5. Try to select students from a variety of social and cultural groups, as well as from various levels of study.

6. Be sure that all peer helper candidates know the amount of time the program will take from their schedule.

7. Inform the parents about the program, first through a newsletter, and secondly, through a letter of permission. Parents are frequently overlooked, but if you keep them informed of events, they will likely be positive and supportive of the program.

Selecting Candidates

Publicity. Publicize the fact that you are recruiting peer helpers. You can do this through bulletins, memos, announcements, and posters. Let all staff and students know of the nomination and sign-up process.

Nominations from Staff. Send out nomination forms to all staff and administrative personnel so that they can recommend students they believe would be appropriate for the program.

Nominations from Students. Ask the student body to nominate individuals they believe would make good peer helpers. List the criteria for nomination, and mention on your list of criteria that nominations can be anonymous. Place the list of criteria, nomination forms, and a closed box (e.g., sealed shoe box with slit) in a high-traffic area.

Sign-Ups. Students can nominate themselves by following the same process followed when nominating others.

Student Information Meeting. Invite all students who have been nominated to attend an information meeting. Detail the goals, guidelines, and philosophy of the program. If your school has an existing peer helper program, experienced helpers can speak to the nominees about their roles and responsibilities.

Questionnaire. Each student who is still interested in becoming a peer helper can take home a peer helper application form (see page 90) to complete, returning it to the school in two days' time.

The Interview Process. Interview all applicants who returned their completed questionnaire. If you are starting a program, conduct the interviews yourself or with the assistance of another interested colleague. If your school already has a program in place, form interview teams comprising advisors and former peer helpers. Create some interview questions (see page 92 for sample interview questions and a rating chart) and decide who is going to ask each question. Review good interviewing techniques. If you have a number of candidates and only a limited number of openings, use the team approach to interviewing and ask three or four applicants to attend the same interview. Either the advisor or a veteran peer helper can outline the program's time commitment. As well, explain that only a limited number of peer helpers can be selected. Emphasize that getting this far in the interview process is exemplary and they should be proud, whatever the outcome.

Follow-Up. Once you have decided on the students who will become peer helpers, advise all applicants of their status by letter. Although time-consuming, it is best if you can also speak with each of the unsuccessful candidates on an individual basis – they have taken part in the process with the best of intentions and need to hear an acknowledgment of their worth. Parents of successful applicants will need to know that their child has become a part of the peer helping program – a separate letter should be sent to the parents to advise them of this information.

Training

It is important that peer helpers know what they can and cannot do. They are not qualified adult counsellors. They must be taught the most effective, empathetic ways of working with people, and should be aware of the social issues and areas of concern, pressure, and stress their peers face. Peer helpers do not have access to student records or guidance facilities unless okayed by guidance or administrative personnel. When faced with a serious student problem that is beyond their range of competence and/or responsibility, peer helpers must refer the client to an adult counsellor.

Most of our training for the volunteer program is done on out-of-school time. Our training schedule includes: three hours on the last day of exams held away from the school, four hours at school during the last week of August, a full day away from the school in September, and two evening sessions of two hours each during the months of September and October at the school.

In terms of the credit program, there are any number of variations. We adapted the program to best fit the needs of our clients and school culture. We wanted to have at least one student available in the guidance office for each period in both semesters, in order that they could welcome new students, assist with tutoring or small-group work, and so on. Training for the group was done during lunch or after school, one day a week for approximately twenty weeks. All credit course peers were expected to attend these sessions, as well as an introductory three-day, two-night retreat in late August.

Whether your group is comprised of volunteer or credit peer helpers, you will find that holding training sessions away from the school to be most effective. Encourage everyone to help, from organizing the training material to food preparation and clean up. Such sessions can be very rewarding. The group develops a special closeness that helps them get through even the toughest times during the year.

Hints for Successful Training Sessions

1. Present the peer helpers with a list of helping agencies and resources within the school and the community. If possible, have speakers from these agencies come in to outline the services they offer, their contact procedures, and so on.

2. It is a good idea for peer helpers to keep a log book or binder containing items such as training information and names of new students.

3. Have your peer helpers keep a daily (or at least weekly) journal that they can share with you at regular intervals. Comment upon, but do not evaluate, their reflections. This is a chance for you to share ideas and communicate on a personal basis.

4. Keep the training simple, interesting, and relevant to your group of peer helpers and the roles they will be required to fulfill. Make it an enjoyable experience.

5. Veteran peer helpers will enjoy running some of the activities during the training sessions, particularly the ice breakers and role plays. Using the veterans in this way will keep them interested and busy, and will take some of the pressure from you. Join in the activities – you can have fun, too!

6. Always supply food!

Roles Performed by Peer Helpers

"Today I showed a new Grade 10 student around our school, helped a Grade 11 student figure out his timetable, and explained to another student and his mother how our peer tutoring program works. With the assistance of two other peer helpers, I also created a bulletin-board display welcoming everyone back to school. Later in the evening, as my friend and I walked home from baseball practice, I listened as she told me how her dad had lost his job because the place where he had worked for twenty years was closing. Patty wanted some ideas on how to help her dad and the rest of her family get through all of this. Her dad is angry and depressed and is really worried about finding another job."

This is a story told by one of my peer helpers about one of the days she came into the school in late August to help with registration, welcome, and orientation of new students. It serves to illustrate some of the roles our peer helpers fill both within the school and beyond.

There are numerous roles or tasks that your group may wish to assume. The following list has been adapted from material published by the Ontario Peer Helpers' Association and serves to illustrate the varied roles these students can play in the school and local community:

- visiting Grade 8 feeder schools,
- conducting Grade 8 orientation and tours of the high school,
- conducting Grade 9 orientation,
- distributing timetables and conducting tours for incoming Grade 9 students,
- conducting orientation sessions with students new to the school, including introducing them to teachers and other students, and answering questions about the school and/or community,
- tutoring,
- assisting students new to Canadian culture or the English language to adapt to the school and the community,
- assisting students in the use of computer-based sources of educational and career information,
- hosting school functions such as Parents' Night, Commencement, and university and college information sessions,
- helping in the guidance office,
- acting as a special friend to students who are experiencing social difficulties,
- helping with special-interest support groups,
- assisting students with study skills, tips for writing examinations, and time management,
- helping senior citizens,
- helping the developmentally delayed,
- initiating special interest/awareness days or weeks regarding various social issues such as violence, abuse, and AIDS,
- extending helping services to community organizations and agencies,
- taking part in peer mentoring,
- taking part in peer mediation and conflict resolution,
- helping, under the direction of special education teachers, selected students who need extra attention and care,
- providing all students with opportunities to talk to caring young people who have been taught to listen with understanding on a one-to-one basis or as part of a small group.

You might wonder how peer helpers can do all of these tasks, especially volunteer peer helpers. Remember that your peer helping program should be specific to your school and its population (review your Advisor's Checklist, page 88). Once you have completed your background research, the roles that you and your peers assume should be geared to the needs of your school and community and available resources.

A Word of Caution...

When you start out, limit your group's responsibilities. Select tasks you feel your group could do a good job with and that will give your group exposure and credibility. Begin small and then expand your program.

Public Relations

The following ideas may be helpful in promoting your group within the school and the broader community.

1. Have the students choose a name for their peer helping group.

2. Design a logo and use it on all print materials related to the group's activities.

3. Ask the group to write an acrostic, a composition where the first letter of each line forms a word or phrase.

4. Create a letterhead and memo pads that peer helpers can use in their correspondence.

5. Make a poster with photographs of all the peer helpers. Post it in a prominent area of the school.

6. With permission from the peer helpers, offer the services of the group to help out at various school functions.

7. Peer helpers can wear name tags, complete with the group's logo, on special school occasions.

8. Make and post flyers in home-rooms and showcases that describe the roles of the peer helpers.

9. Design T-shirts or sweatshirts that can be worn at school and peer helping events.

Here is an exercise to help your group come up with a name. Peers can work as a large group to answer the following questions. They'll need pen and paper in order to complete some of the questions.

1. Our school motto/slogan is...
2. Our school mascot is...
3. Here is a drawing of our school's logo or emblem...
4. These are the words to our school song...
5. The name of our school year-book is...
6. Our school colors are...
7. Our favorite school cheer is...

The peers highlight some of the key words in the school-related information they recorded in the questions. They may wish to use one or two of those words in their group's name.

Ask them to think about the main thrust of their group's responsibilities. They can use the first letter of each word to create an acronym for the group. Here are some examples:

SOS – Students Offer Support (Listowel District Secondary School, Listowel, ON)
PEER – Positive Educational Experience in Relationships (St. Lawrence High School, Cornwall, ON)

Have the peers record some of the roles that their group performs. Using the roles, the peers create an acrostic that describes what the peer helping program can do in their school. This can be an effective device when displayed at school functions, and when acquainting other students and parents of the program's goals. Here is one example to get them started:

Planning, tutoring and study groups to help
Every student who wants to improve his or her grade
Educational and career information explained
Reception and welcome of students new to our school

Funding

You do not need a great deal of money to start a peer helping program, but like any endeavor, it is helpful to have some funds to draw on for advertising and supplies.

You may be able to use guidance materials such as paper, markers, pens, bristol board, and so on for training sessions. You may have to ask the peer helpers to chip in for refreshments or solicit donations from various food establishments such as grocery and convenience stores in return for a service such as snow shovelling, leaf raking, or grass cutting. Service clubs can often be of assistance. A presentation to these clubs on the peer helping program often results in their support.

As your peer helping program evolves, you may find that your group requires funds to initiate and maintain ongoing projects. Funding needs that stemmed from our group's work included:

• sending peer helpers to conferences,
• awarding scholarships at commencement to graduating peer helpers,
• buying inexpensive birthday remembrances for each peer helper,
• purchasing gifts for guest speakers,
• purchasing resources for training sessions and small-group work.

Among the ways we raised funds to subsidize these activities were:

• selling popcorn at lunch time in the cafeteria and at special events such as volleyball, basket-ball, and wrestling tournaments,
• taking part in rent-a-friend days where students "buy" other students or staff members – these friends agree to perform tasks (within limits) the purchaser requests,
• selling Halloween candy bags

and Christmas candy canes – orders are presold and delivered on Halloween and on the day before Christmas holidays begin,
- selling flowers on Valentine's Day.

Other activities include: holding car washes, supervising juke boxes and then splitting the proceeds with the operator, making and selling greeting cards and calendars, and holding bake sales.

The Peer Helping Network

By now, you may have discovered that there are numerous peer helping groups in existence. Elementary, secondary, and post-secondary schools and youth groups, as well as various support groups (e.g., Alateen, Alanon, sexual abuse) use the peer support model as their philosophical base.

It's a good idea to network with similar organizations. You can do this by joining associations, going to conferences, visiting other schools, volunteering your services to help facilitate support groups, and subscribing to peer helping newsletters. If no newsletter exists, you can make your own and then advertise at various community and educational functions for subscribers.

You can start a small network in your area. Are there other schools in your city or town that offer peer support programs? Why not try to organize a full-day or half-day session with them where you share a guest speaker or work on a joint community project?

How many schools in your board or district have peer support programs in operation? We offered a two-day, training workshop (Friday, Saturday) for the eight high schools in our board who had helping programs in place. We held a number of workshops and activities. We had serious time and we certainly had fun time. It was a chance for

advisors to share ideas and concerns, as well as a time for peer helpers to learn, to share, and to get to know one another. It was a worthwhile, rewarding get-together. We want to take part in such an activity again, and hope to include area elementary schools who are interested in the concept of peer helpers.

One of the outcomes of the two-day workshop was the development of a newsletter. Every two months, a different high school is responsible for publishing a peer helping newsletter. We hope to develop our own logo and create a peer helping pamphlet that can be used by all schools to promote the peer helper model.

Organization of a Peer Helper Program

There are numerous tasks that peer helpers may be asked to do in the school and local community. Based on experience, here are my recommendations for success, (your) sanity, and survival: (1) good organization, and (2) delegation of duties.

As our volunteer peer helping program developed and our credibility grew, we kept receiving requests for assistance from various groups, including those of students, staff, administrators, parents, and the community. I felt that we needed to develop a system or method of organization where the peer helpers, particularly the veterans, took on more responsibility. We had to distribute the duties as fairly and as evenly as possible. As a result, we initiated our present system of organization.

The Group and the Working Environment

We have between sixteen to twenty volunteer peer helpers each year. Most of our work is done before or after classes and during lunch time.

Some of the senior peer helpers have a spare period that they may use for peer helping activities from time to time. Our work areas tend to be hallways, locker areas, the cafeteria, the gym, the library, and the guidance office. Unfortunately, we do not have our own office. If a student wants to see a peer helper privately, an adult counsellor's office may be available. For small-group work, we use the reading or waiting area of the guidance office, the library seminar room, or an empty classroom if one is available. Eight to ten students are enrolled in the peer helping credit course.

The Executive

You might find it helpful to have the peer helpers vote in the following positions: President, Vice-President, Secretary, Treasurer, Social Convenor, Public Relations Person, Past-President (if the student hasn't graduated), and Special Events Directors.

In cases where there are existing peer helper programs, the positions should be filled by experienced peer helpers. New peer helpers can volunteer to be directors. You should have no trouble filling these positions as most of the students have a favorite interest and are more than willing to be the director/ co-ordinator for one event.

Planning social functions and acknowledging everyone's birthday with a fun remembrance are the social convenor's priorities. Each year, we leave it up to the new social convenor and advisor to choose how the peer helpers will be remembered. As well, we organize events such as skating, skiing, bowling, and playing volleyball so that the group has a chance to not only work together, but to socialize together.

The public relations person is responsible for all advertising and publicity of our various events. She or he has responsibility for making announcements over the public address system or at assemblies. Other peer helpers may write and/or deliver announcements, but the public relations person has the ultimate responsibility to see that each event is publicized visually and verbally. She or he helps with our newsletter and assists the advisor with community liaison and photo-journalism coverage of many of our events.

Meetings

The entire group meets once a month at lunch time; the executive meets twice a month. Sometimes, however, we may have to have an emergency meeting if we have been asked to do something not already planned. The directors only have to attend the executive meeting if their area of responsibility is being discussed, however, they are always welcome to attend any meeting.

Peer Helpers' Homeroom

If administrators, teachers, or other students need us for any reason, especially an emergency, we gather in a homeroom every morning before announcements. This provides an ideal way to check with the peer helpers and discuss the progress of various events and projects. Morning meetings help to cut down on calling the peer helpers from their classes, and reduce the number of lunch time or after school meetings. As well, this daily contact allows the advisor time to talk with each of the peer helpers on an individual basis and address their needs.

The Calendar of Events

Because we have so many commitments and they seem to come upon us quickly, we developed a calendar of events, which all of the peer helpers receive at the first training session in June. Along with our high school's handbook/calendar that is distributed on the first day of school in September, the peer

helpers plan their time and assess their commitment for each activity. As a sample, I have included a schedule of peer helper events for one year (see page 93).

Working with the Grade 9s

Two peer helpers are assigned to each Grade 9 homeroom. It is their responsibility to visit the Grade 9 homeroom on the first day of school and on a regular basis thereafter – at least once a week.

The peer helpers initially help the Grade 9 homeroom teacher explain the school's calendar of events and help the students complete information forms. They outline the guidance services available at the school, and encourage the students to take part in, and enjoy, Orientation Day.

During the year, as the Grade 9s get to know their two peer helpers, they begin to ask them questions and come to them for help. The peer helpers feel useful, and the Grade 9s feel that they have a couple of friends in higher grades. Many positive feelings and events stem from this peer helper-Grade 9 homeroom match-up.

Special Connections

There are several special programs your group can become involved with, in either a peripheral or indepth manner. These can include: Students Against Impaired Driving (S.A.I.D.), local senior citizens' groups (e.g., shopping for seniors, visiting with a senior friend), and crisis phone lines.

Organizing Special Events

There are special events that peer helpers can organize and oversee during the school year. Examples of these types of events include helping out with registration, offering timetable assistance, and conducting school tours for new students and their families. Peer helpers can do much of the groundwork in terms

of registering a new student and plotting his or her timetable. In this way, the guidance counsellor double-checks what has been done and ensures that both the student's and the parents' questions have been answered.

During this time, older students may want to make a timetable change. Peer helpers can again do much of the groundwork so that the guidance counsellor only has to approve the peer helper's work.

Grade 9 orientation is always an exciting day, and one that peer helpers can take an active part in to make it go smoothly for all. Among tasks the peer helpers can assume are outlining ways to get involved with the school's various clubs and teams and showing a slide show or video of the new Grade 9s which was filmed during their Grade 8 day held the previous spring.

This day – the Grade 8 Tour and Information Day – has proved to be quite successful. In late spring, students of Grade 8 classes pay a visit to the high school so that they will have an idea of what to expect when they begin school in the fall. Peer helpers start the day by inviting the Grade 8s to the gymnasium where they are given a quiz on the school, a door prize ticket, and an information booklet about the school. The Grade 8s are given some time to complete the quiz before being taken on a school tour. Several peer helpers stay behind to mark the quizzes, putting into a box those that have been answered correctly. When the students return to the gymnasium, two prizes are awarded: one is given to the student holding the matching door prize ticket, and the other to the student whose quiz was drawn from the box. The president of the peer helpers introduces the Grade 8s to the student council, the athletic council, various club representatives and the yearbook staff, who answer any questions the Grade 8s may have about the school.

Grade 9 Shadowing

Occasionally, we get a request for permission to send a Grade 8 student to our school for the day. One of the peer helpers takes charge of finding a suitable Grade 9 student who is willing and able to take the younger student with him or her for the day. The guidance counsellor clears the choice of the candidate and gives formal permission. On the day of the visit, the peer helper and the Grade 9 student greet the Grade 8 student in the guidance office before announcements are made. Often the two students will know each other if they have come from the same feeder school.

Letter to Grade 8s

Before the Grade 8s celebrate their graduation from elementary school, our peer helpers send each student a personalized letter that includes their address and phone number in case the student wants to ask them anything about high school. Each peer helper invites ten to twelve Grade 8 students into the high school the week before school officially begins. At this time, the peer helpers take the new students on a school tour and answer any questions they may have. The peers help the Grade 8s get a lock, explain student fees, and let them know what materials they should bring on the first day of school.

Parents' Night

The peer helpers set up an information/promotion booth at Parents' Nights. Peers distribute educational and career pamphlets, explain the resources available to students in the guidance office, and provide information on scholarships and bursaries. In addition, peers outline the tutoring program and have application forms available if parents are interested in getting extra help for their child.

Special Assemblies

At the conclusion of each school year, the guidance department asks the entire school to comment on services provided by the peer helpers. As well, the group asks for suggestions for the next year. Based on the wants and needs of students, our peer helpers try to provide an assembly to meet these requests. One year, there was a high demand for something that would help all students deal with stress.

The dramatic arts students, six of whom were peer helpers, put on a series of scenarios that dealt with stress. A social worker delivered a short commentary at the end of each scenario and explained how an adolescent might handle that particular situation. The assembly was a tremendous hit and the peer helpers felt extremely proud that they had done something worthwhile on a large scale.

Recognition

Given the hard work that peer helpers do in aid of others, it is only fitting that their contributions be recognized at the end of the year. We have found that giving all helpers a certificate at a school assembly to be a deserving public recognition of their efforts. In addition, during commencement, we honor a graduating peer helper with an exemplary peer helper award that consists of a plaque, a certificate, and a cheque. Besides the monetary recognition, the peer gets recognition for his or her work from the audience.

3
Beginning Training

Introduction

You have done all the groundwork and now it's time to begin training those eager young people that you have selected to be peer helpers.

Choose whatever term is best for your situation – helpers, facilitators, supporters, counsellors, mentors, mediators, tutors, or assistants – perhaps incorporating the major roles that your peers will be performing. If assisting with academics is a major focus, the term peer tutors might be best. If you have trained your students in anger management and conflict mediation, peer mediators might be the best name. I did not choose the term "counsellor" since it implies privileged communication and qualified expertise in that area. Our school administration and our students preferred the term "helper" because it encompasses all the roles that they perform and defines how the peers feel about their work with others.

It is important to remember that each group of trainees is unique and develops its own personality. Also, each peer program is unique and develops from needs specific to the group and the school. Your peer helping program and the necessary training sessions will go in the direction you wish to take them.

Pay attention to your students and adapt your sessions to fit their needs and interests. Even though the chapters of this book are presented in a logical sequence for training, I recommend that you re-work the order to suit your situation. Choose the information that you feel is most pertinent to your program and/or group, and put it in the most logical sequence to address those needs.

Our first training session in June, away from the school setting, usually lasts three to four hours. Since the emphasis is on getting to know one another, having fun, and developing trust, I use activities that help us get acquainted, build trust, and that emphasize confidentiality and ethics. Because the peer helpers will be assisting in the guidance office in late August or early September with registrations, school tours, and orientation activities, I also include segments of "Practical Issues: Student Services" in this initial training time.

Session Format

As the advisor, it is imperative that you move step-by-step through each session with your peer helpers. Your experience and professional expertise are necessary to open and facilitate discussions and elicit feelings and opinions, as well as provide important facts and information. Background information of the topics covered in the chapters is provided for your convenience. You can present this material in any number of ways – through demonstrations, discussions, or by student handouts. You are a catalyst who gives students the skills to enhance the qualities they already possess.

Each training session, with some exceptions, follows this basic format:
- outline of session objectives,
- ice breaker,
- description of the new skill,
- practice/completion of the skill by the peer helpers,
- discussion of the skill through questions and activities that enable peer helpers to express their feelings and observations; reflect upon what has been learned; and prepare an action plan if necessary,
- journal-writing time,
- closing activity.

As well, I usually include a review of the previous session's highlights and skills. Journals are of particular benefit at this time as they help peers recall the skills and feelings that were involved in former training sessions. Try to incorporate a few minutes into each session to allow peers time to write in their journals.

Some lessons contain homework assignments, so if you are compressing your training, such as in a retreat setting, you may wish to eliminate those activities that require extended time, research work, or extra resource materials.

Most sessions require peer helpers to write their feelings and/or the feelings that their client experiences. While identifying and describing feelings are not easy things to do, peer helpers must learn and practise these skills. You might consider giving each peer helper a copy of the Feelings Chart (see page 94) to refer to when they are having difficulty identifying feelings.

I have chosen to use the term "client" to designate the person with whom the peer helper is working. We found this term to be less confusing than its alternatives – counsellee, helpee, or interviewee. Your choice of a term will reflect what you and your peer helpers feel is most suitable.

When a Peer Helping Program Already Exists

Let your experienced peer helpers, the veterans, assist you with some aspects of the training. Typically, these students love to "teach" their peers. Be flexible with regard to the training session format. Keep the needs of your group foremost. Sometimes an event or person might need more time or attention, and you may have to cut something short or postpone it until the next time.

The formal training often becomes a part of the final selection process. Excuses for absence and leaving early are good indicators of future commitment. Always be a role model for your peer helpers. If you want them to demonstrate enthusiasm, participation, and respect for others, then you need to demonstrate these characteristics yourself.

Organization is the key! Plan ahead, take a few risks, and share yourself with your peer helpers. Be committed to the program. I am certain that you will find that the enthusiasm and commitment of the peer helpers will make the difficult times bearable and the successful ventures even sweeter. Most of all... have fun and enjoy!

Chapter Sessions and Topics

Detailed here are a listing of the sessions, the topics they explore, and in some cases, advisor's notes outlining special considerations (e.g., need for preparatory work).

Session 1: Getting to Know You (page 19)

Topic: Encouraging Peers to Get to Know One Another

The main purpose of the first training session is to have the peer helpers get to know one another. They will be working together on many group projects – this get acquainted session is designed to help participants feel comfortable with one another.

Advisor's Notes – Getting to Know You

Ice Breaker:
If you think the last person in the circle may have trouble remembering all the names or embarrasses easily, ask the leader to be the last person to introduce himself or herself.

Activity:
Before the peers begin to brainstorm questions they would like to ask their peers, mention that the questions should not be threatening or make a peer uncomfortable. The aim of the session is to increase the peers' comfort level with one another and to make the activity enjoyable.

Discussion:
The Feelings Chart on page 94 lists a range of emotions, and is intended to help peers label their feelings during exercises, as well as those a client may experience. Give each peer a copy of the chart before they begin this activity.

Session 2: Our Group's Guidelines (page 20)

Topic: Making Group Guidelines

Part of building group cohesiveness is building trust. We build trust by getting to know one another so well that we can risk our thoughts and actions with group members. In order to facilitate the building of trust and hence, group cohesiveness, it is important to establish some guidelines for behavior and comment within the group. This session leads the peers through the process of establishing guidelines for their group.

Advisor's Notes – Our Group's Guidelines

Ice Breaker:
As part of this exercise, peer helpers record a fact about themselves that no one else knows. Collect their facts and type or rewrite them in one column on a piece of paper. Make a copy for each peer helper.

As this involves some preparation on your part, you may want to ask the peer helpers to supply their fact to you in advance of the session.

Session 3: I've Got a Friend (page 21)

Session 4: I Am a Friend (page 22)

Topic: Furthering Trust and Confidentiality Within the Group

Getting to know one another through non-threatening group activities, establishing guidelines to facilitate working together, and adhering to the guidelines all contribute to building trust within the group. The two sessions that focus on these concepts have peers working individually, in pairs, and in groups to explore facets of sharing information, confidentiality, and building self-esteem.

Activity:

In this activity, students write an advertisement documenting their qualities as a friend. Given that there is a word restriction (twenty-five words or less), you may find that this is better assigned as a homework exercise.

As well, there is some work for the advisor in this activity. Part of the point of the activity lies in the peers' ability to identify the author of each advertisement, so they will have to be typed or rewritten and a number assigned for identification purposes. When you have typed or rewritten the ads, post them on the wall for display. Make up a master list that matches the ad's number with its author. After students have had a chance to guess the author, you can pass out copies of the master list so they can determine the accuracy of their guesses.

Session 5:
When Is a Promise Not a Promise? (page 24)

Topic: When Problems Are Too Large for Peer Helpers

Students often report that one of their biggest causes of stress is peer relationships – how to get along with others, how to make and keep friends, how to be popular, and how to fit in with a group. As a guidance counsellor, many of the problems I deal with on a daily basis are related to this issue.

As one method of dealing with this problem, I often seek the aid of peer helpers. Why? Teens want teens to listen to them. Peer helpers are closer in age to the distressed teen and may even have experienced a similar situation. The empathetic trained peer helper will be able to listen and offer alternatives to the anxious adolescent that may be more relevant than those suggested by an adult guidance counsellor.

That said, there will always be situations when a problem is too serious for a peer helper to deal with on his or her own. The ability of peers to recognize these problems and to seek the guidance of a qualified adult must be a part of any peer training program. This session offers a true case-study that will help peers recognize that certain situations must be shared with an adult.

Getting to Know You

Interview a partner and then report to the group what you have learned about that person.

Objectives:

▼ to interview someone in your group,

▼ to become comfortable introducing that person,

▼ to learn about other group members.

Ice Breaker:

The Name Game

1. Everyone sits in a circle. As a group, appoint one of your peers as the leader.

2. The leader introduces himself or herself. The person to the leader's right says his or her name and repeats the name of the leader.

3. Continue until the last person says his or her name and repeats everyone's name in the circle.

4. The leader can now ask for volunteers to try to repeat everyone's name. This may be difficult for the first person who attempts this, but you will find that it gets easier as more people repeat the names of the group members.

Activity:

1. Choose a partner, preferably someone you do not know well. If you know everyone, pick the person you know least well as your partner.

2. In groups of six or eight members, brainstorm what you want to find out about your partner, for example:

- nickname,
- age,
- grade,
- number and age of siblings,
- favorite sports,
- reasons for wanting to be a peer helper.

3. Take approximately five minutes to interview your partner using the group's list of questions. You can use the space below to record answers to your questions.

_____

_____

_____

_____

_____

_____

4. Introduce your partner to the group.

Discussion:

1. With your partner, discuss your feelings as you were introducing him or her to the group. Did you feel embarrassed, nervous, proud...?

2. How did you feel when your partner introduced you to the group?

3. How did you feel when you were being interviewed?

4. Record your reaction to the activity in your journal. You can begin by describing how you felt when you introduced your partner and then how it felt when you were introduced to the group. Finish your entry by describing your reaction to being interviewed. Was it fun, or did it make you feel uncomfortable? If you have difficulty finding the right word to describe how you felt, refer to your Feelings Chart. If you like, you can share your journal entry with your partner.

Closure:

Shake hands with your group members and say, "Nice meeting you, Sam, Sara, Anya" and so on. It's okay if you cannot remember a person's name. Simply ask the person to repeat his or her name. Chances are you won't forget the person's name again.

Our Group's Guidelines

This session focuses on sharing information, which leads into a discussion of setting group guidelines. You will have the opportunity to voice your opinions and come to an agreeable conclusion with your group regarding guidelines of conduct.

Objectives:

▼ to facilitate the sharing of information and feelings among the members of the peer helping group,

▼ to establish guidelines that will encourage the building of trust.

Ice Breaker:

Matching Facts and Faces

1. Think about a fact of your life that no one knows about, for example, you have three great aunts or you have visited Mexico four times. Be sure that the fact is something that you do not mind others knowing.

2. Record your fact on a slip of paper, unsigned, and give it to your advisor.

3. Your advisor will type each group member's fact so that no one can identify another's handwriting. All facts will appear on one piece of paper.

4. Try to match each fact with a person in the group. Record the person's name beside the corresponding fact.

5. In a large group, share your fact with the group. Check off correct matches on your piece of paper.

Activity:

As a large group, discuss and develop guidelines for your peer helper training sessions and meetings. Some common rules that typically surface in this meeting include:

- show respect for one another,
- be sensitive to all members of the group,
- maintain confidentiality – what is said in the group stays with the group,
- be one's self – be honest,
- listen to one another and be supportive,
- allow no put downs,
- be on time,
- think positively – try all the activities,
- have fun.

Discussion:

Now that your group has devised a set of conduct guidelines, how will they be carried out or monitored? In small groups of four or five members, devise strategies to ensure that the group's guidelines are upheld. Meet as a large group and pool your strategies. One peer can be in charge of listing and posting the outcome of your discussion on upholding guidelines.

Closure:

Take turns to share with the group what you hope to achieve from taking part in the peer helper training sessions.

I've Got a Friend

This session builds on aspects of trust and openness that you worked on in previous sessions.

Objectives:

▼ to build trust,

▼ to discover what you value,

▼ to discover what others value,

▼ to heighten awareness of the concept of confidentiality.

Ice Breaker:

Tell Me More About You

1. Form small groups of four to six people. The more people in your group, the longer the activity will take.

2. In your journal, record the names of your group members. Under each name leave one or two spaces.

3. Working in pairs, ask your partner to tell you one fact about himself or herself that the rest of the group does not know. Record the fact under the person's name. Switch roles – you now provide your partner with a new fact about you. Change partners so that everyone has a chance to work together in pairs. Remember to tell each new partner something about yourself that you have not told previous partners.

4. Continue until everyone in the group has recorded a fact under each person's name.

5. As a group, you are now ready to share your new facts. For example, Leo is a member of one group. He has been interviewed by the other five members and has told each of the members a different fact about himself. When it is Leo's turn to be introduced to the group, each member tells the fact that she or he learned about Leo. Introduce each member to the group.

Activity:

1. Give yourself a few minutes to think of a secret, something that you have never told anyone because you think it is too private. Hold your secret in your mind for a moment.

2. Now, think of the qualities a person would have to have in order for you to reveal your secret to him or her. Record these qualities in the space provided below.

_____

_____

_____

_____

_____

_____

_____

_____

3. Appoint one of your fellow peer helpers to make a list of these qualities on the chalkboard. Take turns calling out the qualities you recorded.

Discussion:

1. Did you find that most people recorded the same or similar qualities? If yes, what are the reasons for this? If no, outline reasons that could help to explain the different responses.

2. Individually, review the list of qualities you recorded. Are these the same qualities you look for in a friend? Discuss your answers in small groups.

Closure:

Think of a particularly proud or happy moment in your life and write about it in your journal. If you wish, you can share this moment with the rest of the group.

I Am a Friend

Here's a chance for you to become a copywriter. The product to be promoted – yourself!

Objectives:

▼ to enhance self-esteem,

▼ to analyze what you value in a friend,

▼ to discover what others look for in a friend,

▼ to reinforce the group's guidelines for peer helper training sessions, especially trust and confidentiality.

Ice Breaker:

Massage Circle

1. Form a circle where everyone stands shoulder to shoulder. Still standing in a circle, turn to your right.

2. Carefully, place your hands on the shoulders of the person in front of you. Give the person a gentle neck and shoulder massage.

3. When finished, turn to your left and return the favor.

Activity:

1. Here's a challenging activity. In the space provided below, write, in twenty-five words or less, an advertisement that endorses yourself as a friend.

_____

_____

_____

_____

2. Hand your advertisement in to your advisor. She or he will type or rewrite the ads, assigning a number to each ad.

3. Your advisor will display the ads on the wall. Read each ad and try to identify its author. Record the number of the ad and the name of the person whom you believe to be its author.

4. Compare your guesses with the master list provided by your advisor. How accurate were your guesses?

5. Once everyone has had a chance to look at the ads, take them from the wall and make a special book of friendship ads. If you like, you can decorate your ad. You may find that reading through the book is a great activity whenever you feel a little down.

6. Read the poem *A Mathematical Friend* silently. When everyone has finished, elect two of your fellow peer helpers to read the poem aloud to the group. What message do the poets make about friendship? Record your response to the poem in your journal.

Discussion:

1. Form small groups of four or five members. Review what you have learned about confidentiality and what type of person can be trusted with confidential thoughts.

2. Based on your answer to question #2 in the activity section of "I've Got a Friend," is confidentiality a quality you look for in a person with whom you would share a secret? Discuss, as a group, the reasons why this quality is important.

3. Do you think confidentiality is a quality all people expect from a friend or a peer helper?

4. Do you tell all of your friends your innermost thoughts, or do you share these thoughts with only one or two special friends?

5. Discuss the special qualities these select friends share that other friends do not. Do your group members report the same qualities for friends they consider to be discreet and trusting?

6. Have any of your group members had an experience where one of their friends betrayed their trust, that is, told someone something that the person had asked that they not share with anyone? If the answer is yes, they can share how they felt about this experience with the group or record their thoughts in their journal.

Closure:

Write a poem celebrating friendship in your journal. If you wish, you can share your poem with your group.

A Mathematical Friend

A friend should be radical.
They should love when you're unlovable,
They should hug when you're unhuggable,
They should 'bear' when you're unbearable.

A friend should be fanatical.
He should cheer when the whole world boos,
Dance when you get good news,
And cry when you cry, too.

But most of all, a friend should be
mathematical.
He should Multiply the joy,
Divide the sorrow,
Subtract from the past
Add to tomorrow.
Calculate the need deep
in your heart,
And always be greater than the
Sum of all his parts!

Rebecca Tombrook and Kathy Kenyon

When Is a Promise Not a Promise?

Sometimes, you may come across a problem that is beyond your capabilities. In these instances, despite requests for confidentiality, you must report the situation to a qualified adult.

Objective:

♥ to understand the term confidentiality as it relates to peer helping.

Ice Breaker:

1. Divide yourselves into two teams (three, if you have a large group) of equal size.

2. Your advisor will state a category, for example, shoe size, number of people in family, or age. The point of the activity is to determine which group can line up most quickly according to the stated category. You can line up from smallest to largest or largest to smallest.

3. Try the activity a few times. Which team is fastest? Why?

Activity:

Read the following case study silently.

The Dilemma of Sarah

Sarah was an attractive Grade 10 student at a local high school. She lived in a small community fifteen kilometres north of town. Her marks were dropping, she was moody, she quit the basketball team, and wanted to be left alone. Her friends couldn't understand what was wrong with her. One day, in physical education class, her best friend, Kathy, noticed that Sarah was constantly holding her stomach. When she asked Sarah what was wrong, Sarah grimaced and said, "Oh, I must have eaten something bad for lunch." Later, on the school bus going home, Kathy noticed a bruise on Sarah's arm. Kathy asked, "Where did you get that large bruise?"

Sarah stared out the window at the other kids getting off the bus. A stream of tears rolled down her cheeks. "Kathy," she said, "Promise you won't tell anyone, promise! My brother keeps beating me up. Whenever my parents go out, Jim starts calling me horrible, dirty names. When I get mad and tell him to stop, he starts hitting me. He is much stronger than I am, and it really hurts. I've told my parents, but they don't believe me. They just think I get hit playing basketball. Have you noticed I stopped playing? Maybe now my parents will believe me!"

This is a true story. The person to whom Sarah spoke was a peer helper, as well as her best friend.

Discussion:

1. Form small groups of four or five students.

2. In your groups, take turns describing what you think Sarah was feeling when she told Kathy her story.

3. How did you feel as you read the case study? Make a co-operative list of your group members' feelings as you read the story.

4. In Kathy's place, would you agree to Sarah's request that she not tell anyone what has happened to her? Why? Why not?

5. As a group, come up with a definition of confidentiality. Keep in mind that you must define the boundaries of confidentiality so that each member is certain about when a confidence has been broken.

6. Trade your definition with another group. Compare how their definition was similar/different to that devised by your group. Discuss the differences.

7. As a peer helper, you must remember and abide by this important rule at all times, despite the fact that it may cause you to feel uncomfortable:

> **T**here are specific limits to peer confidentiality. **You cannot promise to keep something you have been told a secret if the person is in danger, or if she or he may cause harm to himself or herself, another person, or an object.**

In these cases, you must notify an adult counsellor, a school administrator, a teacher, or an adult who can more capably handle the situation.

When a friend or a client asks you not to tell anyone, you must tell him or her that you can't make such a promise. Your role as a peer helper is to listen and try to offer help to the best of your ability, but if the situation is beyond your control (your friend or client is being hurt, or may hurt himself or herself, someone, or something), you must tell him or her that you are going to speak with a qualified adult.

To ease a friend or client's nervousness, you can offer to go with him or her to see the adult. As well, you can offer to introduce the person to the adult and stay as long as is needed.

Closure:

1. Do one or more of your peer helper colleagues have the qualities you look for in a confidant? If yes, write the name of the person in your journal, as well as a brief outline of the reasons why you think she or he would honor your need for confidentiality.

2. Also in your journal, record answers to these three questions:

- Whenever I tell a friend a secret, I hope...
- Whenever someone tells me a secret, I...
- For me, confidentiality means...

Compare your answers to what you recorded for question #1.

3. This "Dear J" letter was received by a peer helper. Read the letter and her response to the student. How would you have responded? Record a draft in your journal.

Dear J,

I have a serious problem and I don't know who to turn to. When I was young, my dad left my mom and me. Since then, we have been living with my grandparents. Last month, after six years, my father came back to visit and he has been staying with us ever since.

At first I was glad to have my dad back, and I've never seen my mom so happy. It was fun to be a family again until he hit me. We were just joking around, but he got angry and slapped me and called me horrible names. He has done it three times now and I don't know what to do. My mom would be crushed if I told her, and I'm afraid of what my dad would do to me if I ever told. What can I do? I'm scared.

Signed,

Helpless and Afraid

Dear Helpless and Afraid,

You are right when you say that you have a serious problem, and you should not wait to seek professional help. I am willing to listen and do all I can for you, but a problem like this is over my head. I strongly suggest that you tell a counsellor or a staff advisor immediately so they can direct you to the proper agency or person to speak with. Come to me, and we will go to see them together. You are not alone — there are people that can help. Please don't wait until the problem gets worse.

Sincerely,

J

4
Preparing the Peer Helper:
Issues of Self-Esteem and Assertiveness

Introduction

Self-esteem is our own perception of how good (or bad) we feel about ourselves... our belief in our own abilities and how we compare to other individuals.

During my years as a teacher, coach, counsellor, and mother, I have seen that young people who feel good about themselves and have a positive outlook on life tend to have healthy, positive relationships with others, are higher achievers, and are more successful in their studies and activities, both in and out of school. Marion Axford, retired teacher and counsellor "emeritus," states in her book, *Me 'N' You: Go Hug that Kid*, that "self-esteem is the single most important determinant of how a child will progress in school. Until a student feels able, confident, loved, and special, his attention to and learning of the traditional school subjects will be adversely affected" (1993, p. 86).

Everyone's self-esteem needs bolstering at one time or another. It feels good to receive a compliment on a job well-done or on a personal quality. It feels terrible to have someone put you down, especially in front of others.

Exercises in the first part of this chapter focus on enhancing and validating self-esteem in peer helpers, and making them aware of how important a concept it truly is. Hopefully, the peer helpers will take what they learn in the training sessions and apply it, not only when helping others but also in their own lives.

Later exercises focus on assertive behavior. As is evident, the groundwork for assertiveness lies in enhanced self-esteem. Peers, or anyone for that matter, can only be assertive when they acknowledge their own self-worth and view themselves as valuable members of society who have legitimate rights and needs. Discuss with the peers that assertiveness and self-centered behavior are not the same thing: no one has a right to impose his or her needs or wishes when this will cause another person to be treated unfairly.

If peer helpers are to act assertively, it is important that they be aware of certain components of assertive behavior. If they are aware of these components, practise them, and incorporate them into their behavior when working with people, their level of assertiveness will surely improve.

Assertive peer helpers should be able to:

- look directly at the person with whom they are speaking;
- face the person, stand or sit as close as is appropriate, and keep their body and head erect;
- use appropriate gestures, that is, those which enhance the verbal message they send (too many gestures may be distracting to the client);
- have their facial expression reflect the verbal message that they are trying to send. For example, if a peer helper smiles when she or he is in the middle of saying something depressing, the helper will not be taken seriously;
- have their tone of voice, inflection, and the words they use match the message that they are trying to convey;
- be honest, direct, and non-manipulative.

Equally important is the ability to take responsibility for what one says. Assertive language should exhibit "I" statements, not "You" statements. When speaking, assertive people acknowledge their feelings with regard to how the other person's behavior affects them.
Assertive: "I feel angry when you talk to me with that tone of voice."
Non-Assertive: "You make me mad when you yell at me."
Assertive: "I feel embarrassed when you read our marks out loud so all the class hears."
Non-Assertive: "You are really mean when you make fun of me by reading out my mark in front of the whole class."

"You" messages have unmistakable negative characteristics:
- they hurt more often than they help,
- they are used when someone is trying to get another person to change their behavior,
- they are used when a person tries to be superior,
- they are usually a "put down."

Examples of put-down statements include: "You can't do anything right!" "You're crazy to think I would wait for you!" and "You're so unco-ordinated there's no way you would ever be picked for the team."
"I" messages display positive characteristics:
- they do not put down or blame others,
- they encourage honest communication,
- they describe what is going on inside the person.

An "I" message is a non-blameful, non-judgmental way of telling someone how his or her behavior affects others. It consists of three parts:
1. Statement of feelings: "I get upset..."
2. Non-blameful description of behavior: "when you cook something and leave the dirty pans..."
3. Statement of the actual, observable effects that the behavior has on the person: "because I end up having to clean everything."

When peers have finished the sessions in this chapter, they should have a clearer idea of how self-esteem and assertiveness are linked, and how they can begin to help others value and assert themselves.

Chapter Sessions and Topics

Detailed here are a listing of the sessions, the topics they explore, and in some cases, advisor's notes outlining special considerations (e.g., need for preparatory work).

Session 6:
Remember Me As...(page 28)

Session 7:
Self-Validation (page 31)

Session 8:
A Secret Friend (page 33)
Topic: Self-Esteem and Validation

Adolescence can be a difficult and confusing time for teens. The emotional fluctuations and physical changes they experience coincide with a time in their lives when they must begin to think about their future and what they want to do. It is important that involved adults help teens to learn to value themselves and their abilities. Sessions in this section help peers to first identify strengths and weaknesses in their self-esteem, and then plan how they can change some of these weaknesses to strengths.

Advisor's Notes –
A Secret Friend
Activity:
We created mail slots to make it easier for peers to deliver their messages to their secret friends. Give each peer helper a paper lunch bag, ask them to put their name on it, and decorate it in any manner they wish. The "mail" bags can also be used as a repository for regular mail between the peer helpers and yourself.

As well, you might wish to put a time limit on the activity, for example, four months (e.g., from September until Christmas; January to exams).

Session 9:
Looking at Response Styles (page 34)

Session 10:
Exploring Response Styles through Literature (page 35)

Session 11:
Practise Using "I" Messages (page 36)
Topic: Assertiveness

Once the peers have worked on the self-esteem exercises, they will be ready to tackle work on assertiveness.

The first session in this section has peers complete a short quiz that helps them to identify characteristics of passive, self-centered, and assertive responses. In the second session, students apply their knowledge of the three response styles by first finding characters in literature that typify these responses and then developing and dramatizing a scene around these characters. The third and final session has peers practise the use of "I" messages as one way to reinforce their assertive behavior.

Remember Me As...

This exercise provides you with the opportunity to rate your own level of self-esteem – how much you value yourself – through the use of a scale. Once you have determined your level of self-esteem, you can work on an action plan to enhance how you view and value yourself.

Objectives:

▼ to become aware of how you "see" or judge yourself,

▼ to conceptualize (imagine) how you would like to be viewed by others,

▼ to become aware of ways to enhance your self-esteem,

▼ to develop a personal plan of action for enhancing your self-esteem.

Ice Breaker:

I Like People Who...

1. As a group, appoint a leader for the activity.

2. The rest of the group sits on chairs arranged in a circle. The leader stands in the middle of the circle.

3. The leader picks random items or facts and says, "My name is... and I like people who are wearing jeans... wearing the school colors... are taking math this semester... have a part-time job..." and so on.

4. If you fit the category mentioned by the leader, stand up and move to another chair as quickly as possible. The peer left standing with no chair becomes the new leader.

Activities:

1. Complete the self-esteem rating scale, "Where I Stand with Myself."

2. When you have completed the rating scale, reflect in your journal where you stand now with regard to your level of self-esteem.

3. Complete the "Moving Away" activity and the questions that follow it.

4. Form small groups of four or five students. With the group, brainstorm ways to improve your self-esteem. List your suggestions, as well as those made by other students, in your journal.

5. With a partner, develop a plan to enhance your self-esteem. You can serve as a witness to your partner's plan, helping him or her to follow through on initiatives.

Activity 1:
Self-Esteem Rating Scale

Where I Stand with Myself

Rate yourself on a scale from 1 to 5 on the following list of characteristics. Record the number that represents the frequency which you display that characteristic. Here is a description of the scores:

1 – never
2 – occasionally
3 – average
4 – often
5 – always

There are no right or wrong answers to this activity. The most important thing to keep in mind when answering is to be honest with yourself, even when you think the result will not be flattering. Your rating scale is meant to be private and will not be shared with others.

I am:

☐ relaxed		☐ competent
☐ interesting		☐ optimistic
☐ helpful		☐ industrious
☐ confident		☐ a leader
☐ a good listener		☐ happy
☐ modest		☐ creative
☐ enthusiastic		☐ amusing
☐ pleasant		☐ prompt
☐ trustworthy		☐ dependable
☐ friendly		☐ non-judgmental
☐ attentive		

Based on your answers to the rating scale, how would you rate your self-esteem? Circle one rating.

Excellent   Good   Satisfactory   Needs Improvement

Activity 2: Reflection Time

After completing the questionnaire, I feel that I'm the type of person who is

_____

_____

_____

I was surprised that

_____

_____

_____

My greatest strengths are

_____

_____

_____

I learned that I was

_____

_____

_____

I learned that I was not

_____

_____

_____

Activity 3: Moving Away

Suppose that one of your parents has been told by their company that they must transfer to another city or country in order to keep their job. The move will take place at the end of this school year.

Your friends have decided to throw a tremendous going-away party for you. Each of your friends is going to give a short speech about you at the party. What would you like your friends to say about you? Write a short speech about how you would like to be remembered when you move away.

Highlight or underline in red all those qualities that you feel you already possess. Highlight or underline in another color those qualities that you feel you do not possess now but would like to possess.

How I Would Like to Be Remembered After I Move Away

_____

_____

_____

_____

_____

_____

_____

_____

_____

_____

_____

_____

_____

Activity 4: Brainstorming Time

When you have finished, brainstorm with the entire group on ways to improve self-esteem. Nominate one peer to record all the ideas from your session and to make a photocopy for each member. On your own, check the list for ideas that you find appealing for your particular situation. List your favorite ideas here:

_____

_____

_____

_____

Activity 5: A Plan for Improving Self-Esteem

With a partner, develop a plan for enhancing your self-esteem. Remember to be specific. If you want to be a more optimistic person, for example, what things can you do now to work on developing that particular quality? When you are finished, date and record your plan. Share it with your partner or your advisor.

A Plan for Improving My Self-Esteem

Qualities I Would Like to Improve	What Can I Do to Improve?	What Have I Done?
Self-confidence	Volunteer to organize activities, make presenta- tions, help others do things that I'm good at doing	Showed Tammy how to do jump shots at basket- ball practice – Oct. 3 Showed John how to work cash register – Nov. 1

Once a month, meet with your partner or advisor to assess how you are progressing toward achieving your goals. Discuss what you have done to accomplish these goals. Your partner can evaluate your plan and offer suggestions and encouragement, including redefining goals and adjusting timelines.

Closure:

Read the following example of another "Dear J" letter and response. As a group, discuss whether J's reply is the best answer for this situation.

Dear J,

I'm unhappy, lonely, and don't know what to do. My family just moved here because my dad got transferred, and my brother left for university. My mom started working full-time this year, so neither of my parents are home until 6:30 p.m. and when they do come home they are too tired to do anything. I'm in grade nine, I come home every day to an empty house for three hours, and worse yet, I don't even have any friends. Tell me what to do.

Signed,

Desperate Loner

Dear Desperate Loner,

I'm sure these changes seem overwhelming right now. It sounds like you miss your family and you need a little companionship. Maybe it would help to join a club or team at school so that you would be at meetings or practices after school rather than in an empty house. This would give you the opportunity to make new friends, too. Maybe you could volunteer at a day care centre or senior citizens' home. You would be using your free 'lonely' time to help others and probably even have fun! When you are at home alone, try to keep yourself busy to help the time go by faster. Get your home-work done before your parents come home so you can have a bit of free time with them. Why don't you even try making dinner? It will give you something to do, and your mom and dad will really appreciate it.

Sincerely,

J

Self-Validation

Validation means to ratify or confirm something or someone. When we validate ourselves or other people, we recognize that we or they have value. As well, validation is the capacity to see the strengths and positive qualities of ourselves and others. It is the ability to express those strengths when appropriate.

One of the most valuable ways to enhance self-esteem is to give and receive positive feedback or validation. We feel good when people give us honest compliments, acknowledge us, give us a pat on the back, or perhaps even a hug.

Objectives:

▼ to become aware of personal strengths,

▼ to learn to feel positive about yourself.

Ice Breaker:

What's in a Name?

1. Form a circle with all members. One peer can begin by saying his or her full name and telling its history – the source of the name (derivations), and if she or he was named after another person.

2. Many people are given nicknames. If you have a nick-name, either at home or at school, you may want to share it with the group. Some nicknames, however, are personal so don't feel you have to tell others if it will make you uncomfortable.

Activity:

1. Here's a chance to complete a self-validation form. Your form will include five positive things about you, including your favorite photo!

Self-Validation Form

I like the following aspects of my physical appearance:

_____

_____

I am accomplished at these physical feats:

_____

_____

_____

_____

I am good at these activities:

_____

_____

_____

_____

I particularly like these aspects of my personality:

_____

_____

_____

_____

2. Select someone you know well from the group and form partners. Each of you completes a validation form on your partner.

A Validation of My Partner

I like these aspects of my partner's physical appearance and abilities:

_____

_____

_____

_____

_____

My partner is good at the following activities:

_____

_____

_____

_____

_____

I like my partner because:

_____

_____

_____

_____

_____

The qualities that make my partner worth knowing are:

_____

_____

_____

_____

_____

3. Review your self-validation form and then look at your partner's validation of you. Feel free to add any attributes your partner felt you possessed that you did not include on your self-validation form.

Discussion:

1. Is it easier to do a self-validation or validate someone else. Why? Why not? Discuss your response to this question with a partner.

2. In your journal, record a typical response someone gives you when you validate or compliment him or her.

3. Complete your journal entry by describing how you feel when someone validates you.

Closure:

Write a brief journal entry that outlines what you like about yourself.

A Secret Friend

Typically, we are validated by those we know – family members, friends, teachers – but in this instance, you are going to be validated by someone in your group. The catch is, you won't know the identity of your secret friend.

Objectives:

▼ to validate another person,

▼ to have fun,

▼ to demonstrate that peers care about another person,

▼ to contribute to building another's self-esteem,

▼ to get to know another person.

Ice Breaker:

Form small groups of four or five people. Take turns telling your fellow members how you like to be acknowledged or honored on special occasions, or on any day. Your group may find that there are common answers to these questions, including:

- saying hello,
- asking how you are (and being interested in the response),
- congratulating you if you have done something special,
- writing a poem for you,
- treating you to a soft drink,
- giving you a ride somewhere,
- giving you a hug, especially when you feel down.

Activity:

1. As a large group, appoint a leader. She or he writes everyone's name on a small piece of paper and places the names in a container.

2. The leader passes the container around the group. Take a piece of paper, but be careful not to let anyone see the name you have chosen. This person becomes your secret friend. If, by chance, you pick your own name, put the paper back in the container and select another.

3. Once everyone has drawn a secret friend, the real fun begins. You can start to send secret messages, mementos, or inexpensive gifts to your secret friend. To truly mystify your friend, you may ask someone else to deliver your gift. The key to this activity is making the messages positive, fun, and regular (at least once a week).

Closure:

Write a short message of appreciation to your secret friend. Give your message to your advisor. She or he will deliver the letter to your secret friend.

Looking at Response Styles

In order to feel comfortable working with people, you must be able to assert yourself, that is, to stand up for yourself and act in your own best interests without denying the rights of others.

It is important that you understand the difference between assertive responses and other types of responses, including passive responses and self-centered responses. Assertive people demand that their needs are met within reason and without impinging on the rights of another. They believe everyone has equal rights – they do not assume additional rights for themselves.

Objective:

▼ to distinguish between passive, self-centered, and assertive responses.

Ice Breaker:

Positive Feedback

1. Write your name at the top of a piece of notebook-size paper. Leave your paper on your desk or chair, or on a table.

2. Move around the room and write a positive comment on each of your fellow peer helpers' papers.

3. Collect your positive peer comments to read and enjoy.

Activity:

1. Form small groups of four or five members. Review the following list of scenarios. For each scenario, give a passive response, a self-centered response, and an assertive response. One person in your group can record your group's responses.
(a) You are standing in line for a movie. Someone steps in front of you.

(b) You worked with a partner on a project. Your teacher was very pleased with the final product and gives you both an "A." Your partner claims all the credit.

(c) You make plans to meet a friend. He is an hour late and makes no apologies for making you wait.

(d) A friend phones you every day to talk about her problems, which keeps you from doing your homework and chores. You cannot afford to spend so much time on the telephone.

(e) A friend meets you in the hallway at school. He is angry because you were supposed to call him last night at 8:00 p.m. You were playing volleyball and completely forgot to phone.

2. Draw up a list of characteristics for each type of response – passive, self-centered, assertive – based on your answers to each of the scenarios.

3. Meet as a large group and pool your lists. Draw up a master list of characteristics that define each type of response.

Discussion:

1. Return to your small groups and review the master list of characteristics. Discuss reasons why assertive responses are preferable to passive and self-centered responses.

2. Dealing with issues assertively can help you learn to:
- speak up without putting others down,
- listen carefully to the opinion of others,
- accept criticism and compliments,
- deal openly with feelings of anger and jealousy rather than keeping them inside,
- take responsibility for your feelings as opposed to taking them out on others.

In your groups, discuss how your assertive answers to the scenarios in the activity illustrate these points.

Closure:

In your journal, record the type of response you normally use, your level of comfort with it in daily life, and your level of satisfaction with this response in situations that require you to stand up for your rights.

Exploring Response Styles through Literature

In the previous session, you looked at passive, self-centered, and assertive responses. In this session, you will have the chance to explore these response styles through literature.

Objectives:

▼ to find examples of passive, self-centered, and assertive characters in literature.

Ice Breaker:

If...

Form small groups of three. In turn, each member of your group verbally completes the following phrase:

"If I had a magic wand, I..."

Activity:

1. Remain in your groups for this activity. Review the list of characteristics that define each type of response style – passive, self-centered, and assertive.

2. Think of characters you have met in literature, both fiction and non-fiction, that typify these styles of response. Characters can be drawn from literature you are studying in English or French classes, or from books you read as a child.

3. On a piece of paper, record the name of the book in which each character appears, as well as a brief character description. Find an example of a character for each of the three response styles.

4. Write a scene that can be based on an event in one of the books, or develop a new scene. Include your three characters in the scene, and develop dialogue that displays their response styles. Your scene can be sad, humorous, serious, or ridiculous.

5. Dramatize the scene. Ask the other peer helpers to identify the characters you are depicting and the response styles they represent.

Discussion:

In your group of three, discuss the following points. Which of your group members would classify themselves as assertive, sometimes assertive, or non-assertive? How does discussing the following facts help to point out how assertive behavior can make dealing with others in both stressful and non-stressful situations more pleasant and rewarding?

Assertive people, when asking for something or in taking action to get something:

• know what they want, know what their intentions are, and make them clear (i.e., come to the point).

• are straightforward and honest with their feelings and wants.

• speak for themselves and don't tell other people how they should be (i.e., use "I" statements).

• operate with the assumption that other people are equally honest and are capable of saying "No."

• operate within the belief that other people may have differing interests and might say "No."

• have no interest in changing, manipulating, or forcing other people to do as they wish.

Assertive people, when asked to do something or when confronted:

• are capable of saying "No" without undue apologies and excuses.

• accept that they may have different needs and interests from other people.

• don't believe that they have to say "Yes" in order to be liked.

Closure:

Shake hands with your group members. As you shake hands, tell the other person how much you enjoy being his or her "peer helping peer."

Practise Using "I" Messages

There are some simple components of assertive behavior that, when practised and incorporated into your behavior, will make it easier for you to be assertive. One of the most effective and easiest ways of dealing assertively with people is to use "I" messages rather than "You" messages. "I" messages do not blame or label others: they simply tell the other person how his or her behavior makes you feel.

Notice the difference in this example:
Assertive: *I get angry when you don't do your share of the cooking because it means I have to do extra work.*
Non-Assertive: *You're so lazy! You never do anything around here!*

This exercise will give you plenty of practice in using the "I" message formula: I feel... when you... because... .

Objectives:

▼ to practise using "I" messages,

▼ to reinforce assertive behavior.

Ice Breaker:

Today I Feel...

1. In a large group, take turns to describe, in one or two words, how you feel today.

2. Once each person has described their feelings, go around the group again. Members who want to share can tell others why they feel the way they do. For example, "Today I am worried because I failed a test and I don't want my parents to find out." You may choose not to participate if you wish.

Activities:

1. Read the following "You" statements and then turn them into three-part "I" messages. The first message is intended as an example:

- You make me so mad when you are late! You're so inconsiderate!

I feel angry when you take so long to get ready because it makes me late, too.

- You're so lazy! Your room looks like a pigsty – clothes and dishes are everywhere.

_____

_____

- You're so stupid. The other kids laugh at us because of the dumb things you always say.

_____

_____

- You made us lose the game. You're such a klutz!

_____

_____

- You never let me have the car. Don't you trust me?

_____

_____

- You dummy! You made us fail that assignment because you didn't hand it in on time.

_____

_____

2. Form small groups of four or five people. Ask one person if she or he can videotape a segment of a soap opera. Together, you can watch the segment and analyze it for "You" messages – it's almost guaranteed that there will be no shortage!

Write a short script of what you heard and then change the "You" messages to "I" messages. When your script is completed, you can act out for the other groups the original script and then your revised script. Ask audience members to state their reactions to both scripts.

Discussion:

1. Do you agree that "I" messages will help prevent problems in relationships with others? Why? Why not?

2. Do you have a plan for reducing or eliminating "You" messages from your vocabulary? If yes, you can share your plan with fellow peers.

Closure:

Form partners. Using the "I" message formula, tell your partner something you have always wanted to say to him or her since you first met.

5
Attending Skills

Introduction

Attending – paying close attention to what a client says or does – is the basic condition for counselling/helping since it sets the tone of an interview. It shows a client that the helper is listening and is interested in what she or he has to say – the helper cares about the person and the moment at hand.

You may wonder why attending skills are placed before listening skills in this book. From my experience, I have found that new peer helpers find attending exercises to be less difficult and intimidating than listening exercises. This chapter, then, in addition to outlining crucial attending skills, helps to establish a more comfortable environment for the listening sessions that follow in the next chapter.

It is important that peer helpers be aware of how their clients are feeling when they converse with them. Feelings can be expressed verbally in words such as lonely, angry, happy, nervous, and so on. Feelings can also be expressed non-verbally with a smile, a sneer, by gestures, tone of voice, and body language.

As peer helpers become more aware of non-verbal messages and how they may reflect what a person is feeling, they may be better able to interpret what their client is feeling. Remind peers not to be too quick to interpret these messages, however, since cultural, social, emotional, and physiological factors all affect non-verbal communication.

Peer helpers should realize that they can never make assumptions about what their client may be saying or feeling. They should constantly check a situation by asking questions that will help them to clarify what has been said. When peers repeat what they have heard, the repetition can help the client who may discover that she or he has been misunderstood, or that an issue or feeling needs further clarification.

People often disguise their true feelings if they are worried or upset about something; they may act angry or hostile in the hope of getting attention. People who feel inferior or inadequate often bully and act superior to others.

In communicating effectively, it is important to recognize another's hidden feeling(s), to listen to what the person is saying, to find out what that person is feeling, and then to acknowledge that feeling.

Using minimal encouragers is an excellent technique that peer helpers can employ when they want to find out more about what a person may be feeling. Minimal encouragers are those words or utterances that a good attending listener will use to encourage his or her client to continue talking. Examples include: "so," "then," "and," and the repetition of one or two key words "Tell me more," "Give me an example," "Oh, yes," and nodding of the head.

Sometimes, one of the most valuable minimal encouragers is silence. Peer helpers should remember to give their clients time to respond or to continue their story. Silence gives the client time to think, feel, and express exactly what is going on in his or her head. Appropriate gestures and eye contact can be used to support and encourage a client during the silence.

Empathy is the ability to understand another person's feelings and situation. It is being able to understand what she or he is experiencing to the point that the helper is almost part of that person. To use empathy effectively, peer helpers have to be able to recognize the other person's feelings and offer feedback to him or her on those feelings.

It takes practice and concentration to be able to look into and beyond what a client says or does in order to identify what she or he might be feeling. It is important for peer helpers to work hard on developing a personal feeling vocabulary and practising empathy.

To introduce this chapter, ask the peer helpers to imagine that they have something important to tell their friends. They start telling them their exciting news, but soon realize that no one is paying attention. Instead, the friends are busy talking to each other and waving at people passing by. How would the peer helpers feel in this situation?

Next, have the peer helpers make a list of behaviors that they would like to see their friends demonstrate which would make them feel that their friends care about them and what they have to say.

The list that develops might look something like this:
- face the person;
- make eye contact – do not stare – but do look at their eyes regularly;
- demonstrate an open posture, that is, do not fold your arms across your chest;
- lean forward slightly, but do not invade the "comfort zone" of the other person – most people have a comfort zone that they would like others to respect;
- try to ignore distractions and focus on the person;

Read the following poem aloud to the peer helpers. Ask them to discuss, in small groups, how we sometimes lose sight of another person's feelings because of our personal histories and expectations.

I See a Child

I see a child
I see him happy, sad, worried, angry,
indifferent.
I try to be nice,
I try to be understanding.
And he makes me laugh.
He makes me cry.
He disappoints me.
He takes advantage.
I try to see him as he is but sometimes
I react without
      listening.
How can I put aside my own feelings
long enough to see
      through his eyes?
To understand his point of view?
How much of what I see in this child is
coloured by my
      own expectations?
How can I see beyond the obvious?

Cindy Herbert

- relax. Do not demonstrate nervous mannerisms. If you are overly nervous, the other person may also become nervous, making for a very short and ineffective interview,
- use minimal encouragers when appropriate,
- show empathy, that is, try to understand what the person is feeling.

Chapter Sessions and Topics

Detailed here are a listing of the sessions, the topics they explore, and in some cases, advisor's notes outlining special considerations (e.g., need for preparatory work).

Session 12:
Attending Skills
(page 39)

Topic: Attending Skills

How a peer attends to a client will determine the effectiveness of the interview. Peers need help to see how strong attending skills are crucial to effective interviews. This session helps peers to become aware of these skills, and how they can be incorporated into their daily routine.

Advisor's Notes – Attending Skills

Ice Breaker:
This activity is a variation of Charades. Before you use this activity with the peers, print a number of activities, subjects, and places that are related to the school on individual pieces of paper. Fold each piece of paper and place them in a container.

Activity:
On separate cards, copy each of these scenarios. You will need three cards for each triad of students, with each triad getting a copy of each scenario.

Scenario One:
Client talks to counsellor, but counsellor does not pay attention to client. The counsellor should be non-attentive to the point of rudeness.

Scenario Two:
Client talks to counsellor. Counsellor is more attentive, giving the impression of listening to the client, but is still not completely tuned in to the client.

Scenario Three:
Client talks to counsellor who is now very attentive and is listening to what the client has to say.

Session 13:
Non-Verbal Messages
(page 41)

Session 14:
Identifying Feelings
(page 43)

Topic: Identifying Feelings

Feelings can be expressed both non-verbally and verbally. All of us use some combination of the two methods, deliberately or unconsciously. The sessions in this section have peers identify the feelings, both those expressed physically and those expressed verbally.

Attending Skills

By using strong attending skills with a client, you communicate the message that you are giving your undivided attention to him or her. This makes the client feel that you care and that what she or he has to say is important. This session will give you practice in identifying some of these strong attending skills through three distinct role-play situations.

Objectives:

▼ to demonstrate strong and weak attending skills,

▼ to observe and label the feelings that are generated by strong and weak attending skills.

Ice Breaker:

1. Form groups of four or five people.

2. Your advisor will pass a container around each group. Each person takes a slip of paper from the container and keeps its contents a secret.

4. In your groups, take turns acting out what has been recorded on your piece of paper. When someone guesses the item, you sit down.

5. The first group whose members are all sitting is declared the winner.

Activity:

1. Form groups of three. One person will assume the role of the client, the second, the counsellor, and the third, the observer.

2. Your advisor will give the person role playing the counsellor a set of instructions for one scenario. Each scenario should last between two and four minutes. Topics you can explore in the scenarios should be of interest to you, for example, favorite movies and television shows, learning how to drive, and events of the past weekend.

3. After each scenario, peers playing the parts of observer and counsellor record physical behaviors (e.g., facial expressions, body posture, gestures, eye movements) they observed in the client. The client records how she or he felt during the scenario. Your group can use the chart on the next page to record observations and feelings.

4. When the scenario is finished, change roles. The person now playing the counsellor gets the next instruc-

tion card. Continue with the activity until each person in the group has role played the three parts.

Discussion:

1. In your groups, discuss and differentiate between the two areas that arose during the role plays:
- observable behaviors – what behaviors were witnessed, and
- feelings – the thoughts and emotions that were generated as a result of the experience.

2. In a large group, pool your charts and discuss the physical observations and feelings experienced during each scenario.

3. Answer the following questions in your journal:
(a) Which of the client's actions or expressions led you to believe that she or he was uncomfortable during the scenario?
(b) What did the counsellor do (or not do) to demonstrate poor attending?
(c) Other than today's scenario, have you experienced a situation where you were poorly attended? If yes, briefly describe this experience and comment on your feelings during this time.
(d) Now that you are familiar with attending, can you recall a time when you did not attend well to someone? Think about how you might have changed your behavior to demonstrate strong attending skills in this instance.

Closure:

In your group of three, summarize on paper the characteristics of strong attending behavior. Based on your summary, see if your group can come up with an acronym to help everyone remember good attending skills.

Attending Skills: Observation and Feelings Chart

	Observer (client behavior)	Counsellor (client behavior)	Client (feelings)
SCENARIO 1			
SCENARIO 2			
SCENARIO 3			

Non-Verbal Messages

Often our thoughts and feelings affect our non-verbal behavior:

- *We have a sad face and our posture is slumped when we are depressed.*
- *We smile and gesture excitedly when something wonderful has happened to us.*
- *We have a furrowed brow and a pained look on our face when we are worried about something.*

As part of your training, you must become aware of the sometimes subtle but meaningful messages a client may send non-verbally.

Objective:

▼ to become aware of what common non-verbal postures and facial expressions may mean in terms of what a person is feeling.

Ice Breaker:

Mirror Image

1. Form partners. One partner will act the part of the image, the second, the mirror.

2. The image acts out an activity, such as getting ready to go out on a date. The mirror reflects all movements.

3. After a few minutes, change roles with your partner.

4. As you become more practised in reflecting each other, reverse the roles every 15 to 20 seconds. You will eventually become so accomplished at this that it will be difficult to determine who is the mirror and who is the image.

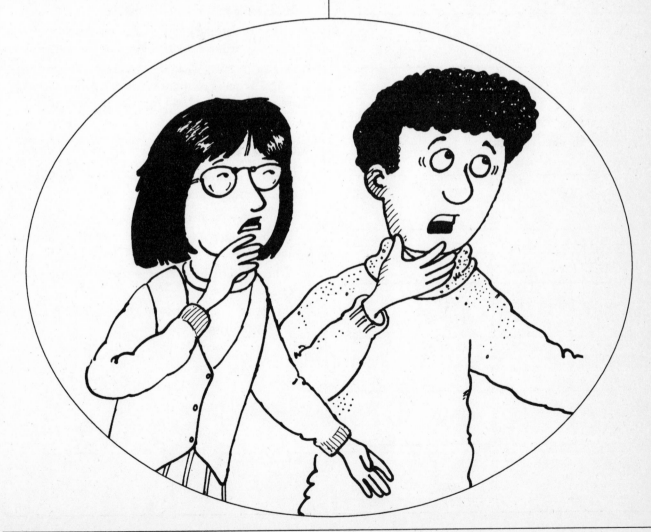

Activity:

1. Your advisor or a volunteer peer helper might like to demonstrate the following examples of body movements and associated emotions. As the performer demonstrates each example, record the emotion you think is conveyed through the following body movements:

Folds arms across the chest:

_____

Wrings or clenches hands:

_____

Stands with legs spread and hands on hips:

_____

Crosses leg, kicks foot slightly:

_____

Strokes chin:

_____

Keeps hands in pockets, directs eyes to the floor:

_____

Covers mouth when speaking:

_____

Raises eyebrows:

_____

Winks eye:

_____

Rubs nose or pulls at ear:

_____

Stares sternly:

_____

Averts eyes:

_____

Constantly clears throat:

_____

2. List or draw some of your own examples of body language and corresponding feelings in your journal. If you need inspiration or are having difficulty naming an emotion, refer to your copy of the Feelings Chart.

Discussion:

1. In small groups of four or five, discuss the different interpretations of body movements.

2. Do you think people "plan" their body language? If yes, give an example to show how and why they would do this.

3. Discuss with your fellow group members how our body language can be inconsistent with how we feel or act. Have you or one of the group members experienced:

- a family member or friend telling the person that she or he is interested in what the person has to say – meanwhile the "listener" is yawning?

- telling something exciting to a parent who claims to be interested but continues to read the newspaper?

4. Are there times when it is good to hide our true feelings? Discuss your answer with fellow group members and give a brief supporting example.

Closure:

Write your answers to the following incomplete sentences in your journal:

- The study of non-verbal messages is...

- From this exercise, I learned that facial expressions and body movements are...

- When I am trying to interpret body language, I must remember that...

- If I am not certain what my client is feeling when she or he talks with me, I...

Identifying Feelings

Now that you have had practice in identifying non-verbal expressions of feelings, it is time to move into identifying verbal expressions. While this may seem easier (at least initially), you may find that some clients are difficult to read, despite their words.

Objective:

❤ to practise identifying and labelling feelings.

Ice Breaker:

"Feeling" Charades

1. Think of a feeling.

2. Form groups of ten. Take turns conveying to the others the emotion that you are feeling.

3. Group members state what they think is the emotion. If they are incorrect, act it out in another way. If members are unable to guess the feeling you are acting out, tell them what you were trying to express.

Activity:

The chart on the next page lists six statements that a client might say to you, a peer helper. Read each statement and record on the chart:

- a word that describes what the client might be feeling, and

- a statement that you might make to the client to show that you understand the feeling.

When you have finished these examples, make up three additional examples. Record your feelings and responses, or trade your examples with another peer helper to answer.

Discussion:

1. Discuss, with a partner, how it is less difficult to label feelings and think about an appropriate response when you have time to read and re-read a statement. It is undoubtedly much harder to label feelings when you are involved in an "emotional" conversation with a client. Clients will tell you if you have labelled their feeling(s) incorrectly. If you say "sad," for example, and the client is mad, she or he will likely set you straight.

2. Label feelings as you listen to the radio or watch television and videos. Record what you saw and heard and report back to your partner. Discuss similarities/differences in your findings.

Closure:

In a large group, take turns saying a feeling word that is not listed on the Feelings Chart. You can use a dictionary or a thesaurus if you wish. Together, you can draw up a class chart that contains feeling words not listed on the chart.

Identifying Feelings

Client says:	Words that describe the feeling	Statement that shows you understand the feeling
"I wore two different socks to school and everyone laughed."	embarrassed, foolish	That must have been embarrassing for You.
"My mother got a job transfer and I have to move to a new city."		
"I got an 'F' in math. My parents are going to be really angry."		
"I want to ask Stacie to the dance, but she probably won't go with me."		
"I felt so dumb sitting on the bench – the coach hardly played me."		
"I'd like to hit Todd – he's such a jerk!"		
"I wish my parents would get someone else to babysit my little sister."		
Example 1:		
Example 2:		
Example 3:		

6
Active Listening

Introduction

Many people think that listening is a simple thing. It isn't. Like everyone, peer helpers need to focus on their listening skills and develop them to the best of their ability.

Generally, it doesn't really matter what a peer helper says or does that helps a client the most – it is showing that she or he cares by taking the time to listen. Listening well, that is attentively, is hard work requiring concentration and patience. To be an active listener, peer helpers must be open-minded and focussed on the person with whom they are speaking. They must keep in mind that they should talk very little, reserve judgment, and refrain from giving advice. The focus of the conversation should be on encouraging the client to talk.

Peers must learn to pay close attention to what a client says. They need to encourage him or her to continue talking, using minimal encouragers such as nodding, establishing eye contact, and asking open questions when necessary. Once the problem has been stated, the peers can begin to clarify the feelings their client is experiencing.

Paraphrasing what a client has said is a useful tool for peer helpers, and one that is beneficial for both the peer helper and the client in the identification of feelings. While it is an important listening skill, you should emphasize to peer helpers that it should be one component of a repertoire that they employ. With practice, such as doing mock interviews, peer helpers will come to know when it is most appropriate to use paraphrasing.

Perhaps the most important point that peer helpers will realize at the end of this chapter is that the best listener does not ask too many questions. Instead, she or he reflects on the thoughts and feelings of the client and offers alternatives.

Chapter Sessions and Topics

Detailed here are a listing of the sessions, the topics they explore, and in some cases, advisor's notes outlining special considerations (e.g., need for preparatory work).

Session 15: Poor Listening Techniques (page 46)

Session 16: Am I Listening? (page 48)

Session 17: Active Listening Techniques (page 49)
Topic: Listening Habits and Techniques

In the first session, peer helpers have an opportunity to display and experience poor listening techniques. This can help them to monitor their own listening practices and to observe and experience the consequences of working with a poor listener.

Many of us are unaware of our own listening habits and, consequently, how these habits impact on those around us. The second session has peer helpers assess their own listening habits in their daily lives. The third session details elements of active listening techniques and gives the peer helpers a chance to contrast negative and positive listening experiences.

In sessions 15 and 17, peers are supplied with lists of listening techniques that can help them pinpoint weaknesses and identify strengths. The lists were adapted from the work of Caroline McNamara, a vice-principal and former head of guidance.

Advisor's Notes – Active Listening Techniques

Ice Breaker:
Before the peers begin this activity, you will need to prepare slips of paper. For each peer, save one, write "Player" on a piece of paper. On the last piece of paper, write "Leader." Place the papers in a container.

Activity:
If possible, have the peer helpers videotape their mock interviews. By now, they are comfortable working with one another and know active listening techniques. Typically, they will not be intimidated by the camera or working in front of others.

Session 18: Listening for and Responding to Feelings (page 51)

Session 19: Paraphrasing Practice (page 53)
Topic: Identifying Feelings

These sessions have peer helpers focus on identifying feelings a client expresses in a conversation. In the first session, peers have the advantage of responding on paper to a series of feeling statements. While this lacks the pressure of a "live" conversation, it helps them to see how feelings need to be reflected back to a client. In the second session, peers again record on paper, but this time by paraphrasing, an effective tool for any peer helper since it has the advantage of clarifying for both parties the feelings the client is experiencing.

Poor Listening Techniques

This session gives you a chance to do something a number of people do unintentionally every day – be a poor listener.

Objective:

▼ to become aware of poor listening techniques in both general and personal situations.

Ice Breaker:

What Did You Hear?

1. Form groups of ten people.

2. One person in each group starts the activity by whispering to his or her neighbor the beginning of a story, for example, "A young boy was walking along the street when... ."

3. The next person continues the story by adding a line, which she or he whispers to the next person.

4. Continue the story until everyone except the last person has added a line. This person repeats what was whispered in his or her ear.

5. As a group, compare the final version of the story to the lines each person added. This can be done by beginning with the person who began the story and moving through the group until the last person says his or her line.

Activity:

1. Select a partner. One partner is to be the student described below; the other, to be the friend the person chooses to confide in. The twist in this activity is that the peer who is to listen should deliberately tune out the troubled friend.

> You are fifteen years old, in Grade 10, and are having difficulty with your school work. All of your friends seem to know what they are going to do after high school, but you don't have any idea. The school dance is coming up and, as usual, you don't have a date, but all of your friends do. You really like this girl/guy in Grade 12 but she/he doesn't know you exist. You really need to talk to someone about these problems, but you are afraid that no one has time or will take you seriously. You finally work up the nerve to talk to a friend about how you feel.

2. At the end of five minutes, the friend rates the helper's non-listening ability on the following "Poor Listening Techniques Rating Chart."

3. Reverses roles and repeat Steps #1 and #2.

Poor Listening Techniques Rating Chart

Employing the following statements as a springboard for discussion, take a few minutes to give your partner feedback about his or her ability to "not listen" to you. Record your estimate of your partner's negative listening skills somewhere on the continuum. Be sure to mention how you felt during the exercise.

Scoring: True = 10   Untrue = 1

	True	Untrue	
1. You avoided making eye contact.	❏	❏	___
2. You interrupted me often.	❏	❏	___
3. You talked more than I did.	❏	❏	___
4. You completely ignored my feelings.	❏	❏	___
5. You gave advice.	❏	❏	___
6. You asked too many questions.	❏	❏	___
7. You sat in a closed position most of the time.	❏	❏	___
8. You kept changing the topic.	❏	❏	___
9. You were more occupied with your other task than with listening to me.	❏	❏	___
10. You often anticipated what I was going to say and didn't bother hearing me out.	❏	❏	___

How I Felt:

_____

_____

_____

_____

_____

_____

Discussion:

With your partner, review the characteristics of poor listening. Think back to the activity. How many of these characteristics did you and your partner incorporate into the role play situations? Discuss each behavior and how it limits effective communication.

Closure:

Record in your journal how you felt when you role played the part of the client. Describe the impact of a counsellor's poor listening habits on a client.

2. **Adopts closed physical posture, for example, folds their arms over their chest, crosses their legs.**

1. **Avoids eye contact.**
(*Note:* Eye contact is unacceptable in some cultures. If you find that a client is avoiding eye contact because of a cultural belief, ask the client about it. If you would rather not ask the client, excuse yourself for a moment so that you can consult an adult counsellor.)

3. **Interrupts.**

4. **Anticipates what the speaker is going to say and, as a result, misses what was actually said.**

5. **Changes the subject.**

9. **Talks about own experiences.**

6. **Performs a second task while person is talking.**

10. **Is oblivious to speaker's feelings.**

ARE YOU **LISTENING?**

7. **Gives advice.**

11. **Confuses facts with opinions.**

8. **Ignores speaker.**

12. **Asks too many questions.**

Am I Listening?

This session may hold some surprising discoveries for you concerning your own listening habits.

Objective:

▼ to assess personal listening habits.

Ice Breaker:

"Simon Says"

1. Form a large circle.

2. One person can volunteer to be the leader, Simon. She or he will call out actions such as: run on the spot, tap a person on the shoulder, open the door, touch your toes, laugh out loud, and so on.

3. There is a catch to doing the activities. Follow the command only if the leader says "Simon says" before the command. If the leader doesn't include "Simon says" before the command, do not follow his or her instructions.

4. The game becomes more difficult when the leader issues commands quickly. You must listen carefully to what she or he says.

5. The last person standing (in addition to Simon) is the winner.

Activity:

Mark on the following quiz how often you do each activity. Record one of three categories when answering:

    0 – Never
    1 – Sometimes
    2 – Almost all the time/all the time

____ 1. I let others finish speaking before I talk.

____ 2. I look at the person who is speaking.

____ 3. I'm more concerned about understanding others than convincing them that I'm right.

____ 4. I ask questions to clarify my understanding when I'm not sure.

____ 5. I pay attention to the way things are said to help me understand.

____ 6. I wait until I get all the instructions before I leave to do something.

____ 7. I am open to new ideas.

____ 8. Others think I am a good listener.

____ 9. I pay attention to non-verbal messages.

____ 10. I make sure that others know I understand them.

____ 11. I try to listen while doing something else that also takes my attention.

____ 12. I'm more concerned about my point of view than the other person's.

____ 13. I change the subject when someone is in the middle of saying something.

____ 14. I ignore what others are saying.

____ 15. I'm too busy to listen carefully.

____ 16. I use subtle or nonverbal questions to let people know I really don't want to listen anymore.

Discussion:

1. Points 1–10 are examples of strong listening skills; points 11–16, examples of weak listening skills. Ideally a good listener will score 2 on points 1–10 and 0 on points 11–16. Based on your answer to the quiz, do you think you are an active (good) listener or a poor listener?

2. With a partner, discuss what you think are the attributes of a good listener.

3. Record these attributes in your journal. As well, rank yourself according to whether you are an active listener or a poor listener. If you think you are a poor listener, can you and your partner list activities and tips that might help you improve your listening skills?

Closure:

Review your responses to the quiz. Circle the number of any statement that you think represents an area you need to work on.

Active Listening Techniques

Unlike the last session, you will want to display excellent listening and attending skills in a helping situation.

Objectives:

▼ to practise active listening,

▼ to evaluate personal active listening techniques.

Ice Breaker:

The "Frozen" Handshake

1. Take a slip of paper from the container your advisor passes around the group. Do not show other members what your paper says.

2. With one exception, members' papers will read "Player." Recorded on one piece of paper, however, is the word "Leader."

3. Mingle and shake hands with one another. While shaking hands, the player with the paper "Leader" secretly squeezes someone's hand very tightly. This person becomes a "Freezer."

3. The "Freezer" moves through the crowd, shaking hands. As she or he shakes one person's hand very tightly, the freezer also winks at the person. This person is almost frozen. To prevent instant identity, the victim counts to ten silently and then, dramatically, freezes on the spot.

4. Anyone not frozen can guess the identity of the Freezer by saying, "I know who the Freezer is. It is... ." If the guess is correct, the game starts over with a new person again selected by the leader mingling about shaking hands and squeezing a player's hand tightly.

5. If the person who guesses is incorrect, she or he must freeze. The game continues.

6. The object of the game is for the Freezer to see how many people she or he can freeze before being identified.

Activity:

1. You will need to work in groups of three for the activity. One member will assume the role of the client, another the counsellor, and the third, the observer.

2. Your group will hold three mock interviews so that each person has a chance to play the other parts. Here

are suggestions for topics that can be explored in the mock interviews:

- the importance of friends,
- what school means to you,
- future plans,
- major accomplishments,
- getting a driver's licence,
- volunteering.

3. Assume your roles and select your topic of discussion. Each interview should last between five and ten minutes.

4. In each interview situation, the observer checks off the appropriate areas on the following Active Listening Behaviors Chart.

Active Listening Behaviors Chart

Place a checkmark beside those traits you observe in the counsellor during the mock interview.

_____ faces client

_____ maintains eye contact

_____ leans forward

_____ maintains open posture

_____ has a relaxed body posture

_____ gives full attention to the client

_____ nods head in agreement occasionally

_____ smiles

_____ uses minimal encouragers

_____ acts naturally

_____ encourages client to talk

_____ tries to understand feelings

Overall Rating Circle one:

Needs Improvement   Good   Excellent

Discussion:

In your group, discuss each person's rating chart. Did one or more of you have difficulty maintaining some of the active listening techniques? If yes, discuss together how this behavior may be improved. Remember that everyone can probably improve his or her listening skills to some degree, so do not be too harsh in your assessment of another's listening abilities.

Contrast this session with the session where you experienced poor listening techniques. In your role of client, record in your journal how this session was more profitable for everyone involved. Review the list of characteristics and benefits of active listening and identify those behaviors that you witnessed in this session.

Characteristics of an Active Listener

1. Wants to hear what client has to say.

2. Wants to be helpful.

3. Is able to accept person's feelings.

4. Is able to trust the person's ability to cope with his or her feelings.

5. Is able to respect the person's ability to work through his or her problems.

6. Is able to accept the fact that feelings are transitory.

7. Is able to accept the fact that the person is unique.

Benefits of Active Listening

1. Encourages a person to become less afraid of revealing negative feelings.

2. Promotes warmth in a relationship.

3. Encourages a person to talk.

4. Facilitates problem solving; an individual eventually develops skills for solving his or her own problems.

5. Influences the individual to be more willing to listen.

Closure:

Complete these sentences in your journals:

• When I took part in the poor listening session, I...

• Practising mock interviews makes me...

• I feel that I need to practise...

Listening for and Responding to Feelings

By now you realize that an essential part of communicating effectively is recognizing and acknowledging the feelings of others. In this session, you will have the opportunity to further develop active listening techniques that involve listening for feelings.

Objectives:

▼ to practise the labelling of feelings,

▼ to practise the construction of active listening responses.

Ice Breaker:

Play "Simon Says" again to help you determine if practising the active listening techniques from the previous session increases your success at this game.

Activity:

1. Look at the examples below of poor and active listening.

2. With a partner, discuss each of the statements on the next page and decide on the underlying emotion. Together, form an active listening response by incorporating the feeling into the response.

Discussion:

With your partner, review your responses. Discuss the difference between having the time to think of a response (writing) with being in an interview situation (talking). No doubt, you find it much easier to have time to formulate a response on paper – most of us do – however, the more you practise active listening techniques, the easier you will be able to identify a client's feelings.

Closure:

Review the following list of common mistakes many of us make when listening. In your journal, record the opposite, that is, a corresponding active listening technique.

1. Sounding like a parrot or a robot.
2. Talking about content only – ignoring feelings.
3. Giving cheap advice.
4. Using poor attending skills. You sound good, but you look like you don't care.
5. Shifting attention to yourself. Talking instead of listening.
6. Having no energy.
7. Sliding into non-helpful replies such as joking, making judgments, reassuring, and so on.

Poor Listening

Student Says	Peer Response	Feelings
"I hate the teachers at this school! They don't care about kids."	"That's not a very nice thing to say. I think that some teachers really care."	• feelings are ignored

Result: Increased anger and frustration – possibly channeled into hostility toward listener. Person feels as though peer is preaching to him or her.

Active Listening

Student Says	Peer Response	Feelings
"I hate the teachers at this school! They don't care about kids."	"It sounds as though you are really angry."	• angry • upset • frustrated

Result: Communication.

Client Says	Client Feels	Active Listening Response
"I really studied hard and I still failed chemistry."		
"I really hate school. I'm quitting as soon as I turn sixteen."		
"My parents fight all the time. They don't even think about my brothers and me."		
"Sally gets asked to every dance. What's she got?"		
"There aren't any decent guys/girls in this school."		
"My mother treats me like a baby. Nobody else has to be in by 11:00 p.m."		
"I'd like to try out for the team but I won't make it."		
"I finally passed a math test."		

Paraphrasing Practice

Paraphrasing is a helping technique that has the helper attempt to feedback to the client the general idea of what she or he has said. It has three purposes:
- *to convey to the client that you are trying to understand what she or he is saying,*
- *to summarize the client's comments by repeating what she or he has said in a concise manner, and*
- *to check your perception to make sure you understand what the client has said.*

Here is an example of a client's statement and a peer helper's paraphrased response:

Client: *"My parents always take my brother's side. They think he can do no wrong."*

Peer Helper: *"You feel that your parents favor your brother."*

Objective:

▼ to practise the helping skill of paraphrasing.

Ice Breaker:

The Forbidden "I"

1. Form partners. If you do not have a partner, you will be the leader. If there is an equal number of peer helpers, the advisor will be the leader.

2. The leader tells everyone what the start signal will be. As well, she or he assigns the topic to be discussed, for example, the latest assembly, last weekend, a part-time job, or a current event.

3. The leader gives the signal and tells everyone the discussion topic. The stipulation of the discussions is that no one is allowed to use the following words: "I," "me," "my," or "mine." If you use one of these words, you must remove yourself to a separate spot in the classroom.

4. The leader claps his or her hands every 20 to 30 seconds to signify that the partners must change. In the instance where one partner has been disqualified, the other partner must wait until the change before resuming the activity.

5. The winner is the last person left.

Activity:

1. Form partners.

2. Together, create a paraphrasing response for each of the following client statements:

Client: "I don't know why I am failing this course. I do my homework and study for tests."

Helper: _____

_____

Client: "The coach made me sit on the bench the whole game just because I missed practice."

Helper: _____

_____

Client: "My sister always wears my clothes. I told her to stay out of my room, but she goes in and gets my clothes after I leave for school."

Helper: _____

_____

Client: "My parents won't pay my car insurance. Why did I even bother to get my driver's licence?"

Helper: _____

_____

Client: "I was late for work and my boss told me off in front of all the others."

Helper: _____

_____

Discussion:

With your partner, discuss your level of comfort when using this technique. Many people find that when they first begin to paraphrase, they feel like they are acting like parrots, mimicking what the client had said. Once you practise this technique a number of times, you will come to realize that you do not have to repeat exactly what was said, rather you simply emphasize and summarize the words of the client.

Closure:

In your journal, list words or phrases you can say to the client to lead into using the paraphrasing technique, for example, "Correct me if I'm wrong. Are you thinking that..." "Let me see if I understand what you have been saying..." and "If I hear you correctly, you're saying... ."

7

Facilitative Responses

Introduction

When someone is referred to a peer helper or personally seeks him or her out for help, what should the helper say to that person to show that she or he cares?

It is sometimes difficult for anyone – professional counsellors, peer helpers, friends – to determine what is best said in certain situations to encourage the client to talk and provide the information the listener needs in order to help.

Studies of verbal behavior in counselling, psychotherapy, and teaching indicate that there are many kinds of responses. Robert Myrick and Tom Erney, in their books *Caring and Sharing* and *Youth Helping Youth* have identified six response styles that can be treated in relation to the area of peer helping. Some of the responses are more helpful than others and for this reason are presented here from the least to most facilitative:

1. Advising and Evaluating

2. Analyzing and Interpreting

3. Reassuring and Supporting

4. Questioning and Probing

5. Clarifying and Summarizing Events

6. Reflecting and Understanding Feelings

All of these responses, at one time or another, can be facilitative. No single response can be classified as good or bad, effective or ineffective. Rather, peer helpers must consider the situation, the timing, and the probable effect the use of that response will elicit. They need to know, however, that some responses tend to be more facilitative than others in building a helping relationship.

On Myrick and Erney's "Continuum of Facilitative Responses" (1979, p. 44), the authors encourage peer helpers to focus on the high facilitative responses – Questioning and Probing, Clarifying and Summarizing Events, Reflecting and Understanding Feelings – and use them as much as possible during counselling sessions.

On the pages that follow are overviews of each of the responses and the situations where they can be most effectively used.

1. Advising and Evaluating

An advising or evaluating response implies what the helper thinks the other person might, ought, or should do. Giving advice is one of the most common and easiest responses we give when someone comes to us for help. It's a familiar response we have learned over the years from our parents, siblings, teachers, and friends. Instead of trying to help a client take responsibility for decisions, the helper, when using this response, automatically gives him or her advice, as though the situation or problem belonged to the helper. The helper advises the client on how she or he would handle the situation; the client follows the advice, thinking that the helper's way is the best or only way to handle it. When a helper evaluates the situation as to what she or he would do, the advice removes all responsibility from the client for making a decision.

If the advice is threatening or unwanted, such as in a disciplinary situation from parents or teachers, the response will be resistance or even hostility. When a client is having a problem, the last thing she or he wants is to be made to feel inferior, which is precisely what happens when the helper tells the client what to do. The client may get the impression that she or he is being "talked down to" from someone intent on showing superiority.

If a peer helper feels that an advising response is best for the situation at hand, it is imperative that she or he take time to completely understand the problem. If advice is given quickly, the client will feel that the peer helper does not want to take the time to listen. From a counselling or helping standpoint, the helper has taken on the problem and has not taught the client anything about learning how to make decisions and accept responsibility for himself or herself.

When advice is given as a referral to other people or sources of information and not as a final solution to a problem, it can sometimes be of great benefit to the client.

Client: "I need a part-time job and I don't know where to begin to find one."

Peer Helper: "Maybe you could go to the employment office and fill out an application. I think, though, that it might be best for you to first talk with the guidance counsellor."

Evaluation also makes us think defensively. This is true even when it is positive. When people evaluate our work, there is a tendency to think some of the following thoughts:

- They think I am...
- They want me to...
- They probably won't like it if I...
- They probably won't take it as if I...
- I guess that means that they are... and I am...

Some parents and teachers use advice and evaluation in an attempt to encourage young people to do something. When praise (evaluation), for example, is used to motivate, there is a tendency for the recipient to believe that certain expectations must be met before she or he is of value. The process of producing to please others is often a self-destructive one that offers little personal fulfillment.

Although there are pluses for this response, advice and evaluation should be rated low in terms of enhancing communication.

2. Analyzing and Interpreting

As the name suggests, people who use this response try to analyze a client's behavior and feelings, and then tell the client why she or he is behaving in a certain way. Often, the listener is only making guesses. Trish Loraine (1985) states that analyzing and interpreting is one of the hardest responses to use effectively since it requires a great deal of thought, knowledge, and experience.

Recipients of this response may become defensive and reluctant to communicate what they are thinking or feeling since few people like to be told such things as, "The reason you don't like... is because.." or "It's easy to figure out why you are unhappy." Most people prefer that the listener help them understand their feelings, rather than tell them why they feel as they do.

Analyzing and interpreting is a response that should never be rushed and used only when the listener is extremely sensitive to the client's feelings. With the exception of professional counsellors – psychologists and psychiatrists – this response should be used as little as possible.

3. Reassuring and Supporting

These responses should be used with caution. Even though they are given with the idea of offering support and encouragement, they often communicate a lack of interest or understanding because of their generalized nature. Examples of these responses include: "Nobody's perfect," "Everyone feels that way," "Time heals all wounds," and "Tomorrow is another day." Ask the peer helpers to list more clichés or generalizations that they have heard.

Support and reassurance denies the client's feelings. When helpers use this response, they imply that what the client is feeling is perfectly normal and so common that she or he should not be concerned with it.

It's important that peer helpers remember that everyone has a right to feel the way they do. As helpers, they must treat their client's feelings with respect and importance. They must honor the clients by really listening and helping, and not just offer them empty clichés and generalizations.

4. Questioning and Probing

There are various types of questions that a peer helper can use when trying to elicit information during an interview, discussion, or conversation. Asking effective questions is an important skill for a peer helper. Many people feel that they know how to ask questions, but they often make mistakes in their choice of the type of question that is appropriate for the situation.

Peer helpers must be particularly careful when asking "why" questions. To begin, these questions may force people to justify their behavior and are often seen as criticism. When asked, they sometimes generate negative feelings and give clients the sense that they must defend their behavior or opinion.

The use of "what" and "how" questions is preferable to that of "why." When a client is asked "what," "where," "when," "who," and "how," they are given the opportunity to be more precise in their response. These questions are typically less threatening than "why" questions and do not force the client to be on the defensive.

Closed questions usually get short answers, such as "Yes," "No," or "I don't know." They usually force a specific answer, thus giving the client a feeling of a "third-degree interrogation" if they are used continuously. They may also make the client feel that the helper is prying into areas that are off-limits. An example of a closed question would be "Why didn't you do your assignment?"

Open-ended questions, on the other hand, can encourage clients to talk about themselves and elaborate on the reasons why they are seeing a helper. These types of questions also give the client the impression that the helper is genuinely interested in what they have to say because the helper encourages them to talk. An example of an open-ended question would be "Can you tell me what part of the assignment was difficult to understand?"

Informational questions ask the client to respond by giving facts. These questions are not intended to elicit elements of emotion; rather, a listener will ask such a question when she or he needs more information to determine how or why a client may be feeling a certain way. An example of an informational question would be "How old were you when your parents divorced?"

Feeling questions are exactly that – questions that ask the client how she or he feels or felt about a person, event, or object. The answers elicited by such questions assist the peer helper in identifying the feelings of the client.

An example of a feeling question would be "How did you feel about the exam?"

Once your peer helpers have had experience in asking questions you might like to try this method with them. Ask the peer helpers to make a statement rather than ask a question. This is a good way to get a client to talk or to encourage him or her to keep talking. The statement can either:

(a) call for an answer, or

(b) be a reflective statement that does not interrupt the communication and is simply used to clarify or summarize what the client has already said.

Read the example below and then have the peer helpers change the remaining questions into statements.

Question	Statement
What do you want to be?	Tell me about your career plans.
Do you have a part-time job?	_____
What did your teacher say?	_____
How many people are in your family?	_____
Are you going on holiday?	_____

With practice, your peer helpers will grow increasingly confident and competent in their questioning techniques.

5. Clarifying and Summarizing

This response is used to highlight the most significant ideas or events mentioned during a conversation or an interview. There are two types of situations where this response is used:

(a) when the helper is not certain about the client's thoughts or feelings, she or he can use a clarification statement to check what has been said, for example,

"From what you've said, it seems that..." or "Tell me if I'm wrong, but are you thinking that...."

(b) when the helper wants to provide feedback to the client on what has been said, that is, to give him or her a chance to hear what she or he has actually been saying.

This response gives clients a chance to confirm or correct the summary, as well as to change or correct what she or he has said. For example, "You've mentioned two concerns. One was... and the second was... ."

The clarifying and summarizing response is one that peer helpers should use often. It not only clarifies what the client has said during the discussion, but also reassures the client that the helper has followed his or her ideas and is trying to understand the situation and the client.

6. Reflecting and Understanding Feelings

Feelings can be expressed through words, non-verbal behavior, and paralinguistic factors (qualities of voice such as tone and pitch). Thus, peer helpers must listen to how the client speaks. For example, the client may speak quickly when communicating enthusiasm, but more slowly when communicating discouragement.

Empathetic peer helpers strive to go beyond the ideas that are expressed by their clients to the feelings that accompany the words. The helpers actually hear the feelings, try to label them, and then reflect these feelings back to their client.

Before beginning with the response styles, review with the peer helpers the value of the following techniques when in a counselling situation:

• minimal encouragers,

• empathy,

• strong attending skills,

• tuning into the client's feelings.

Discuss how each of these components can play a crucial role in developing and maintaining rapport with, and trust of, a client.

Barriers to Effective Communication

"Communication stoppers are helper behaviors, which although they appear to be helpful, are really responses that are negative in effect and retard helpful interpersonal relationships." (Tindall & Gray, 1985, p. 59).

The following discussion of communication stoppers (or blockers) is adapted from the work of Judith A. Tindall and H. Dean Gray in their book *Peer Power: Becoming an Effective Peer Helper* and from Rey Carr and Greg Saunders in their book *Peer Counselling Starter Kit*.

Each communication blocker shares the same negative qualities:

• puts down client,

• doesn't solve problems effectively,

• doesn't help to make client feel better,

• weakens communication because client tends to withdraw from helper.

There are eleven common and destructive communication blockers, including:

1. Advising

The helper gives his or her answers to others as a way to solve the problem.

"Why don't you..."

"What I would do is..."

"There's only way to handle that..."

Hazards:

• prevents a client from working through his or her problem,

• can cause dependency on the part of the client,

• may make the client angry or hostile.

2. Moralizing or Preaching

The helper tells the client things that she or he should or ought to do.

"You should..."
"You ought..."

Hazards:
- may create guilt feelings and put client on the defensive,
- client will resist if she or he doesn't agree with helper's way of thinking (e.g., "Who says I have to do it that way?").

3. Ordering and Commanding

The helper tells the client to do something without giving him or her a choice.

"You must not feel that way..."
"You have to..."

Hazard:
- often creates anger and resentment on the part of the client since few people like to be told what to do.

4. Warning or Threatening

The helper tells the client that if his or her behavior continues, it will result in certain consequences.

"You'd better, or else..."
"If you don't stop, then..."

Hazards:
- can cause the client to feel anger, fear, and resentment,
- often induces the type of behavior which is exactly opposite to what is desired.

5. Arguing or Persuading

The helper tries to influence another person to think as she or he does.

"This is the way it is..."
"Statistics say..."
"Yes, but..."
"You are wrong because..."

Hazards:
- may cause client to feel inferior,
- often causes client to turn inward and "clam up,"
- may also cause client to stop listening,
- may result in counter-arguments (e.g. "So what?").

6. Criticizing, Judging, Blaming

The helper makes a negative interpretation of the client's behavior.

"You're lazy..."
"You are not organized enough to..."
"You're too insensitive to..."

Hazards:
- implies the client is not as bright as the helper,
- puts client on the defensive and induces feelings of inferiority,
- client may accept the helper's judgment and really believe what the helper has said,
- may foster retaliation in the client (e.g., "I'm more sensitive than you are.").

7. Praising and Agreeing

The helper makes a positive evaluation of someone's behavior.

"You always say the right thing."
"You look great in that color."
"You were playing a great game! I know why you're mad at the coach for taking you off the floor!"

Hazards:
- client may see this response as being insincere and manipulative (i.e., praising so that client will perform desired behavior),
- may cause client to worry that she or he cannot live up to the praise the helper has given.

8. Name-Calling, Kidding, Teasing

The helper tries to avoid talking about the problem by laughing or distracting the client.

"Not bad for a dummy like you!"
"What a 'browner'."
"That's too bad about your cousin. I've got a great joke that will take your mind off your troubles."

Hazards:
- negatively affects a client's self-image,

- often causes verbal and perhaps physical retaliation,
- does not help to solve problems,
- hinders communication.

9. Analyzing or Diagnosing

The helper analyzes the client's behavior and lets him or her know that the helper has "figured them out."

"You're acting that way because you're tired."
"You must be drunk... you're not making sense."
"What's really wrong with you is..."

Hazards:
- client can become upset and frustrated,
- client may become fearful that the helper will read more into his or her behavior than is wanted.

10. Supporting, Reassuring, or Sympathizing

The helper tries to talk the client out of the way she or he feels, or to deny the existence of the feeling.

"Don't worry, things will get better."
"I know just how you feel."

Hazards:
- causes the client to feel misunderstood,
- may make the client feel guilty for worrying about something,
- may sound nice, but is of no help in solving the client's problems,
- leads to hostility because of its denial of feelings.

11. Changing or Diverting the Subject

The helper changes or diverts the subject brought up by the client.

"Let's not talk about such depressing things."
"You think that you've got problems, you won't believe the kind of day I've had."

"Let me tell you about the trouble that I had with English."

Hazards:
- may make the client feel that his or her problems are unimportant,
- suggests that life's problems are to be avoided and not discussed.

Chapter Sessions and Topics

Detailed here are a listing of the sessions, the topics they explore, and in some cases, advisor's notes outlining special considerations (e.g., need for preparatory work).

Session 20: Working with the Four Main Types of Questions (page 59)

Session 21: Questioning Practice (page 61)

Topic: Questioning

Familiarity with the four main types of questions will assist peers in counselling sessions. Asking the right question at the right time is a key counselling skill and one that can do much to enhance the effectiveness of an interview. The first session provides peer helpers with the chance to become acquainted with the four main types of questions and to experiment with using the questions. In the second session, peer helpers can employ the four types of questions in a counselling situation and record the frequency and effectiveness of each type of question.

Session 22: Clarifying and Summarizing (page 63)

Session 23: Recognizing Feelings (page 64)

Session 24: "The Squid" (page 66)

Topic: Recognizing Feelings

Peers have had several sessions where they have provided clients with feedback regarding their feelings, both those expressed non-verbally and verbally. In the first two sessions, peers focus on using the clarifying and summarizing response as the primary tool for feedback, and recognizing and labelling feelings. The third session introduces peer helpers to a new tool for recognizing feelings – "The Squid."

Advisor's Notes – Clarifying and Summarizing

Activity:
This is an excellent exercise to demonstrate the very reason why we must understand and reflect back feelings to clients. If we can get different answers from these straight-forward questions, imagine the misinterpretation and confusion that could arise during a fifteen-minute interview session.

Advisor's Notes – "The Squid"

This activity was developed by Sid Allcorn, a founding member of the Ontario Peer Helpers' Association. He used this effective learning activity with his volunteer and credit course peer helpers.

Session 25: Recognizing Barriers to Effective Communication (page 69)

Topic: Communication Barriers

All of us employ communication barriers, whether or not we are aware of them. This session helps to make peer helpers aware of how they use communication blockers in interactions with others. They are encouraged to spot the use of blocks and eliminate their use in sessions.

Working with the Four Main Types of Questions

There are four main question types: open, closed, informational, and feeling. In this session, you will be provided with examples of each and will have the chance to employ the four types of questions.

Objectives:

- to become familiar with four common types of questions,
- to discover the best type of questions to use in a counselling situation.

Ice Breaker:

Guess the Celebrity

1. Together, make up about forty cards with famous characters written or drawn on them. Place the cards in a container.

2. Form partners. Both you and your partner take a card from the container and tape it to your partner's back. Do not tell your partner what the card on his or her back says.

3. Take turns asking each other questions about the character on your back. There is one stipulation when asking questions – you can ask only closed questions (questions that elicit "Yes" or "No" answers).

4. The winner is the first person to correctly guess the character on his or her back.

Activities:

1. Read the following examples of the four question types.

Closed:

"Do you like school?"
"Can I use the phone?"

Open:

"What do you like most about school?"
"What troubled you about the exam?"

Informational:

"When did you start high school?"
"How old are you?"

Feeling:

"How do you feel about going to high school?"
"If you were a parent, what would you do?"

2. Now, read the following example of a closed and open question. In both instances, the person wants to find out how the client liked the school dance. Notice the difference between the two questions. With a partner, role play this example to illustrate the answers that are possible in both instances.

Closed	**Open**
Did you like the dance?	What did you like about the dance?

3. With your partner, practise forming open-ended questions by taking these closed questions and turning them into open-ended questions.

Why aren't the dishes done? _____ _____ _____?

When are you going to do your assignment? _____ _____ _____?

Are you shy? _____ _____ _____?

Where did all your money go? _____ _____ _____?

Why do you want the car? _____ _____ _____?

How could you forget your homework again? _____ _____ _____?

4. List the characteristics that you think define each type of question.

Closed

Characteristics: _____

_____

_____

_____

Open

Characteristics: _____

_____

_____

_____

Informational

Characteristics: _____

_____

_____

_____

Feeling

Characteristics: _____

_____

_____

_____

_____

Discussion:

1. With your partner, discuss and record in your journal the type of questions you feel are most suitable to the counselling situation.

2. List the reasons why you feel these types of questions would be most effective.

Closure:

Think about a small child who always asks the question "why" each time the child's parents try to explain something. How do you think the parents feel after three or four "whys?" Now, think about how a client would feel if you constantly asked, "why?"

Questioning Practice

Now that you are acquainted with the four main types of questions, you can put your knowledge to use by testing them in a counselling situation.

Objectives:

▼ to practise using a variety of question types,

▼ to observe and analyze the best types of questions to use in a counselling situation.

Ice Breaker:

Finding Favorites

1. Record on a sheet of paper the name of your favorite television show.

2. For the next five minutes, circulate around the group and ask questions to find others who liked the same show.

3. When you find someone who likes the same show, ask what she or he particularly enjoys about the program.

4. When everyone is finished, take a poll to identify the most popular television show and the reasons why the majority of peer helpers like it.

Activity:

1. Form groups of three. One member will take on the role of the interviewer, the second, the client, and the third, the observer.

2. For three to four minutes, the interviewer asks the client about how things are going at school, or what that person likes to do for fun.

3. (a) On the chart on the next page, the observer records the various types of questions that the interviewer uses and the general effect of these questions on the client.

(b) The observer also checks off the number of times each of the four main question types was used. If the observer thought that there was a combination of question types used, she or he checks off both areas. As an example, if the interviewer asks an open-feeling question, then both the open and feeling categories would be checked.

4. Change roles so that each member has a chance to play the observer, client, and interviewer.

Discussion:

1. As a group, discuss what you feel to be the best type of questions to use in a counselling situation and why you feel this way. Is your response similar to that given in the Discussion section of the last session?

2. (a) When you were in the role of observer, did you notice the client exhibit any change in facial or body expression? If yes, with what type of question(s) did you note this change?

(b) Did the client's facial expression and/or body movement give you, as the observer, the impression that she or he was reacting positively or negatively to this type of question?

3. As the interviewer, did you change the type of question you asked based on the client's responses? As an example, if you asked a closed question which did not elicit the required response, did you follow it with an open or feeling question?

4. In your role of interviewer, did you experience a situation where your client was not saying very much? What did you do? Give an example.

5. Did you, as the interviewer, use the client's answers to generate further questions? (This is an indicator of good listening skills.) If yes, give an example.

Closure:

Complete these sentences in your journal:

• Before learning about the various types of questions, I used...

• Now, when asking my peers questions, I...

• When someone asks me questions, I wish she or he would...

Observer's Chart

Interviewer: _____   Client: _____

Question Types	Number of Times Used	Effect on Client
Closed:		
Open:		
Informational:		
Feeling:		

Clarifying and Summarizing

When you clarify and summarize a conversation or interview, you highlight the most significant ideas or events that have been mentioned. You can use this response in two ways: (1) to check what a client has said and (2) to provide feedback on what has been said to that point. In both instances you offer the client a chance to clarify or change what she or he has said.

Objective:

▼ to practise the skill of clarifying and summarizing.

Ice Breaker:

1. Draw a face (a simple circle with eyes, nose, and mouth) that symbolizes how you feel today.

2. Put your name on your picture and then leave it on your desk or chair, or on a table.

3. Walk around the class, look at each of the drawings, and write on each person's drawing what you think is the emotion represented.

4. When everyone has commented on the drawings, review the comments on your picture to see if the guesses of the other peer helpers were correct.

Activity:

Read the following scenarios. In your journal, record your clarifying and summarizing response to each of the four scenarios.

Scenario One:

I want to drop one of my classes. The teacher hates me. Right from the start in September, whenever anything happened in class, I got blamed. If he has his back to the class and someone starts talking or making noise, he always blames me. He picks on me constantly and it's not fair. I want to drop the class.

Scenario Two:

My parents always let my sister do anything she wants to and they don't let me do anything. She gets to go out through the week and if she wants to have people in, she can. I can never go out, no matter how important it is. If I want to have a friend overnight, I have to clear it with my parents a week ahead of time.

Scenario Three:

My friends had this big party planned on the weekend at someone's house and I guess they took great pains to keep it quiet because I never knew a thing about it. I certainly wasn't invited. I don't know what's going on – all of a sudden they don't want me around.

Scenario Four:

There are some kids in this school who gang up on me and make me feel like a fool. They get into my locker and rig it up so my books all come crashing out when I open it. They hang around and insult me and call me names. In the cafeteria, they make a point of sitting next to me so they can do mean things.

These scenarios were developed by Jay Clayton-Ross, head of guidance at a youth centre in Ontario. Clayton-Ross gives the following responses to illustrate the clarifying and summarizing approach:

1. "You feel you've been treated unfairly and you are angry and fed up."
2. "You feel there are separate sets of rules for you and your sister and you don't get equal treatment. You feel resentful of this unfair treatment."
3. "You feel left out and that hurts you."
4. "For some reason, a gang of kids is making your life miserable at school. You feel angry and wish you could get them to stop."

Discussion:

With a peer, review your responses to the four scenarios to those of Jay Clayton-Ross. Were your responses similar or different? If they were different, discuss what you believe are the reasons that would account for this difference.

Closure:

Record your own scenario. You can give it to one or two other peer helpers who will try to clarify and summarize what you wrote.

Recognizing Feelings

Here is a final practice session that focusses on recognizing feelings.

Objective:

❤ to practise recognizing feelings.

Ice Breaker:

Smile... I Like You

1. Form a large circle. One helper can volunteer to be "It." The task of "It" is to make someone smile when she or he is not supposed to.

2. "It" goes and stands in front of a peer and says, "I like you. Won't you smile for me?" The peer replies, with a straight face, "I like you too, but I cannot smile." If the peer does not smile, "It" repeats the procedure with another peer. If the peer smiles, the two exchange places and she or he becomes "It."

(Note: "It" can make faces, do contortions, sing, dance – almost anything that she or he wants to do – with the exception of physical contact.)

Activity:

1. Read the following statements to yourself. In the space labelled (a), write the word or phrase that describes what you think the person is feeling.

• My mother and father have been fighting a lot lately.

(a) _____

_____

(b) _____

_____

• I wish my Geography teacher would quit picking on me.

(a) _____

_____

(b) _____

_____

• I don't know if we can trust him.

(a) _____

_____

(b) _____

_____

• My mother has to go into the hospital.

(a) _____

_____

(b) _____

_____

• They think I stole money from the locker room.

(a) _____

_____

(b) _____

_____

• I won second prize.

(a) _____

_____

(b) _____

_____

• My sister always gets what she wants.

(a) _____

_____

(b) _____

_____

• Why can't I have the car?

(a) _____

_____

(b) _____

_____

3. Form partners. Your partner reads each sentence aloud. In (b), record the word or phrase that describes what you think your partner is feeling as she or he reads each statement.

Discussion:

1. With your partner, compare your responses. Were your answers the same of different? If they were different, which questions elicited a different answer from that of your partner?

2. Do you think that tone of voice, body language, and/or facial expressions are responsible for the difference in answers?

3. Do you feel that you are getting better at labelling feelings? If yes, explain why in your journal.

Closure:

Reflecting and understanding feelings is an excellent response to use in any counselling situation. It takes practice and concentration, but once mastered, will be one of your most valuable tools.

Review the following points with your partner:

- Listen carefully to what the person is saying and how she or he says it.

- Be aware of body language, eye movements, and paralinguistic behavior.

- Remember the content (what the client is talking about) and the feelings (the emotions they are experiencing).

- Do not rush replies. It is not necessary to respond to every statement. Pauses work well and give the client time to compose his or her thoughts.

- Do not project personal feelings on to the client. Verbally reflect the client's feelings only.

- Always use strong attending skills.

Given these points, can you and your partner come up with a suitable acrostic?

"The Squid"

Here is a challenging activity that will help you to further refine your skill of identifying facilitative responses.

Objectives:

▼ to identify the types of responses that encourage conversation,

▼ to identify the types of responses that discourage and may alienate a client,

▼ to see which type of response you prefer to use.

Procedure:

1. Read each situation and then circle the number of the answer you feel is most appropriate (facilitative).

2. Beside each response, record which type of facilitative response you think it is:

S = **Supportive:** reassure and pacify – danger of taking over with own experiences

Q = **Questioning:** who? what? – draws person out, danger of taking over the conversation

U = **Understanding:** empathetic

I = **Irrelevant:** changes flow of communication to accommodate what the helper wants to talk about, changes focus from client to helper

D = **Directive:** tells person what to do, solves problem, analyzes client's behavior, points out right/wrong, good/bad in client's actions

---

A. "It doesn't seem to matter what I do, it's wrong. If Mom isn't mad at me, Dad is. Do the dishes, take out the garbage, do your homework, clean up your room, get off the phone, pick up your clothes, and on and on and on. I'm going to quit school, get a job, and move into an apartment. I've had it."

1. ____ You're not alone. There are probably a lot of students in this school that feel the same way.

2. ____ Have you felt this way only recently? Do you have to do the dishes very often?

3. ____ A few more weeks of this and you've had it.

4. ____ Amen. Let me tell you about my family.

5. ____ Maybe your parents think this is for your own good. Eventually you'll have to do those things on your own. This is good training.

B. "My foster home isn't bad, but I really miss my parents. I know I wasn't very good at home, but I love my mother. I may be allowed to go home for Christmas. My mother is very sick."

1. ____ Well, I'm sure if you behave yourself now and do what you're told, you'll be allowed to return home.

2. ____ Hang in there – you can do it.

3. ____ What bad things did you do when you were home? Do you like your foster parents?

4. ____ You're very worried about your mom.

5. ____ I'm glad you're talking about foster homes. There seems to be so many government-run homes around now.

C. "I really want to do well in school. I know it's important, but I just can't seem to get down to work. What can I do?"

1. ____ I'm glad you came in. I have been trying to see you about those library books you have out.

2. ____ Lots of people have good intentions. Maybe you only say you want to do well and are not willing to make the necessary sacrifices.

3. ____ There are lots of students who feel the same way. Give it time – I'm sure things will improve.

4. ____ What do you mean by well and what things have you tried?

5. ____ You're really worried about your school work.

D. "I've been in this school now for five months but I don't know anybody. I can't seem to make friends. I try to be friendly, but inside I'm really uncomfortable. I try to convince myself that I don't care, that I don't need anybody anyway and I've almost come to believe it."

1. ____ You've been a very lonely person.

2. ____ That reminds me of a song I heard the other day, something about "it's great to be lonely 'cause that's how I met you."

3. ____ Maybe you should consider joining a club in the school that would get you to meet other people.

4. ____ I'd like to be your friend. You seem friendly.

5. ____ When you first meet someone, how do you act? What do you say to them?

E. **"What's the use of staying in school? My friends who have left are having a lot more fun. They have money and girl friends. I really hate coming to this place every day."**

1. ____ How many friends are like this and are you sure they're happy?

2. ____ You really hate this place.

3. ____ Girl friends. Now there is an interesting topic. Talk about a mess. Wow, if you ever get girls figured out, let me know.

4. ____ I understand how you feel about that, but it's going to keep you from getting anywhere if you don't try to get away from it.

5. ____ Lots of people feel the way you do – sometimes with good reason. You'll forget it as time goes on and you get things going again.

F. **"My boyfriend and I have had a fight and I'm afraid we might break up."**

1. ____ You'll both get over it. Maybe it will strengthen your relationship.

2. ____ When did you have the fight?

3. ____ You're really upset.

4. ____ Isn't that a coincidence? We just did too.

5. ____ Well maybe you should stick to your guns this time and get somebody new.

G. **"My parents always give my little brother anything he wants. Then they won't give me anything. It's not fair."**

1. ____ Why don't you speak up for yourself and tell them?

2. ____ It's probably your imagination. Your parents would never do that.

3. ____ Does your brother notice the difference?

4. ____ You feel cheated because you aren't getting what you think you should in your family.

5. ____ I'm glad you brought up the topic of brothers. My brother is not so little and he is still a pain.

H. **"I cheated on the math test. The answers were staring me in the face and I just copied them down."**

1. ____ That's an interesting moral question. I can see both sides of it.

2. ____ Have you thought about just telling the teacher you cheated. She would appreciate your honesty.

3. ____ Hey, don't worry about it. Everybody does that once in a while.

4. ____ Where were the answers?

5. ____ Sounds like you're feeling a little bit guilty about it.

I. **"I want to stay away from drinking but the temptation is too great. I'm around it every weekend."**

1. ____ Sounds like you are uptight because you are afraid of yielding to temptation.

2. ____ Speaking of drinking, are you going to the dance this week? I heard everybody was going!

3. ____ Why don't you make some new friends who don't drink?

4. ____ Everybody drinks these days.

5. ____ How often do you drink? What do you drink?

J. **"I didn't mean to say the wrong thing. Anna is just so sensitive to everything."**

1. ____ What did you say?

2. ____ You seem upset because you really had no intention of hurting her feelings.

3. ____ Being sensitive can cause a lot of hurt – just ask me.

4. ____ Why don't you apologize?

5. ____ Some people are impossible to get along with. Just be glad you are rid of her.

K. **"I can't make up my mind about what to do after I get out of school. I don't want to go to college and I don't want to keep the same job I have now for the rest of my life."**

1. ____ There are lots of young people in the same boat.

2. ____ What is your job?

3. ____ You're worried about the future and don't have any ideas at all.

4. ____ Isn't it awful these days? Unemployment is so high.

5. ____ You should take an interest survey to find out what you want to do.

L. "My father and mother were yelling at each other until 4:00 this morning. I didn't get much sleep last night. And I'm supposed to turn in a five-page report today. I don't know what I'm going to do."

1. _____ Go and see the teacher about it and explain.

2. _____ Hang in – things will look better tomorrow. You aren't alone.

3. _____ What were they fighting about?

4. _____ You're kind of worried about your report and your parents.

5. _____ This isn't the first marriage I've heard of breaking down.

Directions:

1. Under the appropriate letter, record the number of the answer for each question that you feel fits the type of response.

2. Circle the number that you chose as your answer for each question.

3. Tabulate how often you chose each response style.

	S	Q	U	I	D
A.	....	....	....	....	....
B.	....	....	....	....	....
C.	....	....	....	....	....
D.	....	....	....	....	....
E.	....	....	....	....	....
F.	....	....	....	....	....
G.	....	....	....	....	....
H.	....	....	....	....	....
I.	....	....	....	....	....
J.	....	....	....	....	....
K.	....	....	....	....	....
L.	....	....	....	....	....

Discussion:

1. Which response style did you use most often in this exercise?

2. Did you feel that you frequently use this style in everyday situations?

3. In small groups, discuss and compare your answers with those given below. Remember that all answers are open for discussion and that you may come up with points to justify answers different from those given.

	S	Q	U	I	D
A.	1	2	3	4	5
B.	2	3	4	5	1
C.	2	4	5	1	3
D.	4	5	1	2	3
E.	5	1	2	3	4
F.	1	2	3	4	5
G.	2	3	4	5	1
H.	3	4	5	1	2
I.	4	5	1	2	3
J.	5	1	2	3	4
K.	1	2	3	4	5
L.	2	3	4	5	1

Closure:

In your journal, write an example of each of the "SQUID" responses for the situation given below.

"I don't think I'm going to pass this year. I study for all the tests but I never pass them. What should I do?"

S: _____

_____

Q: _____

_____

U: _____

_____

I: _____

_____

D: _____

_____

Recognizing Barriers to Effective Communication

Most, if not all of us, have found ourselves in situations where we have stopped another person from communicating with us. Often, we do this unintentionally – we say or do something that inhibits the person and makes him or her withdraw from us. In this session, you will have the chance to analyze your conversation for use of communication blockers (or stoppers), and to try to limit their use in your dealings with others.

Objective:

▼ to identify your use of communication blockers in conversation.

Ice Breaker:

Group Mechanism

1. Form groups of five or six members.

2. As a group, think of a moving machine, and then attempt to imitate it (e.g., a washing machine, bicycle, blender).

3. Demonstrate your marvellous machine to the other groups. They can try to guess the identity of the machine.

Activity:

1. Form partners. With your partner, come up with a list of scenarios that you might encounter as a peer helper, for example, a student is having trouble with another student, or a student is failing a class. One of you can assume the role of a peer helper; the other, the client.

2. Role play the situations. The partner playing the client can stop the role play when she or he feels that the peer helper has blocked the conversation. For example, a peer helper tells the client that she or he shouldn't dislike another student. In this instance, the peer helper is telling the client how to feel. Chances are that the client will not want to continue the conversation.

3. As you continue to role play the situations, record your use of communication blockers.

4. Switch roles and repeat the activity, using new scenarios.

Discussion:

1. With your partner, discuss how you respond when someone blocks your communication. How does your partner respond? Are your responses similar or different? If they are different, try to outline the reasons for this.

2. Were you surprised by the type or number of communication blockers that arose during the role play situations? If yes, describe to your partner what most surprised you.

3. Discuss and record situations that prompt you to use communication blockers.

Closure:

If you would like to change your style of communication, try this exercise. For one week, take a count of the number of times and in what situations you tend to use communication blockers. Record your findings in your journal. At the end of the week, after you are aware of where and when you use these ineffective devices, make an effort to change your style of response. Ask your advisor and your fellow peer helpers for assistance with monitoring your communication and providing suggestions for alternate ways of handling situations.

8
Decision Making

Introduction

Peer helpers have practised the techniques of good attending, paraphrasing, summarizing, reflecting feelings, and using open-ended questions to elicit information. They are now ready to contribute even more to their counselling sessions.

Decision making is a key skill that peer helpers must be taught. It is a skill that they in turn will teach or at least reinforce with their clients.

At this point in the peer helpers' training, they have learned and practised how to listen to the problems and concerns of others. They are aware of and understand the importance of empathy. These helping skills, however, are sometimes not enough and the client may need help in learning how to make good decisions.

One model that has been designed to help people make major decisions is that of Myrick and Erney (1978). Comprising five steps, this model takes a person from the initial step of identifying the central issue or problem through evaluating the results of a decisive action by:
- identifying the central issue or problem,
- exploring the issue or problem and the alternatives and consequences,
- choosing a next step,
- acting upon a choice,
- evaluating the results.

Here is an example of a decision made following this five-step plan.

Aaron has always wanted to become a medical doctor. As you know, math and science are very important for this career. Unfortunately,

Aaron is experiencing difficulty with his Grade 11 advanced math. He has failed his last two tests and has lost confidence in his math ability. The final exam is only one month away. Aaron is really worried and doesn't know what to do. He has come to a peer helper for assistance in making a decision.

Step One: Identify the Problem

The simplest way to identify the problem is to turn the concern into a general question. Thus, Aaron asks, "What should I do about my math work?"

Step Two: Explore the Issue or Problem

With Aaron, the peer helper explores all aspects of the problem by considering the following:
- alternatives,
- relevant information,
- criteria,
- consequences.

Alternatives
Aaron's peer helper can use the brainstorming technique to list as many alternatives as possible, for example:
- drop level of the course,
- if fail the course, repeat it,
- drop the course,
- get extra help from the teacher,
- get extra help from a tutor,
- if fail the course, go to summer school.

Relevant Information
Collect relevant data on each of the alternatives.
- Can Aaron get into medical school if he takes a lower-level math course?

- How much money will a tutor cost?
- Will he have to spend an extra semester in high school if he repeats the course?

Criteria
From this information, important factors emerge than must be considered in the selection of best alternatives, for example:
- career goal,
- chance of success (realistic assessment of ability),
- diploma requirements,
- parental pressure,
- enjoyment of course,
- accuracy of mark (could teacher's evaluation be incorrect?),
- peer pressure.

Consequences
Aaron and his peer helper must consider the consequences of each alternative. As well, they need to consider the short- and long-term effects – not only what the decision means at the present, but what it will mean for Aaron in the future.

An easy way to explore and assess all this information is to draw up a simple chart. From the list Aaron and his peer helper generated from brainstorming, they can choose the best (most realistic) choices or alternatives. Now, the two write in these possible alternatives as column headings. They record the criteria as row headings (some criteria may come from their list of alternatives). For example, if achieving a career ambition is a valid point for one of the alternatives, then the two may wish to compare all the alternatives with regard to a career goal.

Step Three:
Choose a Next Step

Aaron and his peer helper now need to weigh the alternatives on the basis of the criteria. Before picking the best alternatives, they must use their criteria with each alternative to decide which best answers the question.

To help them do this, they need to add up the information in some way. One of the simplest methods to do this is to use plus and minus signs. If an item would be an advantage (positive), they put a plus sign in the box. If they feel an item would be a disadvantage (negative), they put a minus sign in the box.

If they want to give some criteria more weight, they use a ranking system where the most important criteria are assigned a "3," average criteria are assigned a "2," criteria that have little value are assigned a "1," and criteria that have no value are assigned a "0." When using a numerical ranking, they put a "+2" if the item has a positive value (an advantage) or a "-2" if the item has a negative value (a disadvantage).

As was evident by the total rating, Aaron decided that getting a tutor for math was the best alternative for him.

Step Four:
Act Upon a Choice

Aaron has chosen his course of action and now takes the step of implementing the plan. He found a tutor with the help of his math teacher. His parents offered to pay for the tutor as long as Aaron worked hard to improve his math mark.

Step Five:
Evaluate the Results

This final step involves assessing the outcome of Aaron's decision. He has acted upon his chosen alternative and has experienced its consequences. Is he satisfied with the results? His personal value system will probably come into play as he evaluates the results of his decision. Is this decision good for Aaron and for the other people it affects?

If the alternative Aaron chose does not prove to be the best one for the situation, then he can go back, with the aid of his peer helper, and examine the factors that led to his decision, re-evaluate, then choose another alternative, thus making a new decision.

It was easy for Aaron to evaluate his decision because it was completely objective: either his marks improved or they did not. If his math marks went down, he would have to choose another alternative. Because of his determination to pass the course, he worked hard and co-operated with his tutor at every step. Needless to say, he passed his math course. In addition, with the excellent review of mathematical skills he received from his tutor, he went on to pass the subsequent math courses he needed for entrance to university.

Much of this chapter focusses on working with this simple yet effective decision-making model. There are more sophisticated and detailed models in existence, as there are higher levels of decision making. If peer helpers choose to follow these five simple steps, their decisions will be planned and based on the

	Drop Level of Course	Repeat Course	Drop Course	Extra Help – Teacher	Extra Help – Tutor	Summer School
Career Goal	-3	+1	-3	+3	+3	+3
Chance of Success	+3	+3	0	+3	+3	+3
Diploma Requirements	0	+1	-3	0	0	0
Parental Pressure	-3	-1	-3	+3	+3	-1
Like the Course	0	0	0	0	0	0
Accuracy of Mark	0	0	0	-1	0	0
Peer Pressure	-1	-1	0	-2	0	0
Total Rating	-4	+3	-9	+6	+9	+5

most relevant data for their client's particular situation. Once they have practised using the model, they may wish to learn more about higher-level decision making. The resource list on page 96 lists some titles the peer helpers may find useful.

It is important to remind the peers of the following facts:

- not all problems can be solved,
- not all people want help with their problems,
- we each own our own problems and are responsible for our actions. No one else can solve our problems for us.

Peer helpers need to keep in mind that if they take over a client's problem, the client will have learned nothing about problem solving and decision making. The client may feel relieved at the time, but may blame the peer helper if the solution proves incorrect. Even worse, the client may become dependent on the peer helper for future decisions. The goal for an effective peer helper must be to help others find the solution to their own problems.

By the end of this chapter, peer helpers will have completed one of the most important segments of their training. They have learned the most helpful responses when working with a client in a helping/counselling situation. The summary on the next page can be given to the peer helpers as an overview of their work.

Chapter Sessions and Topics

Session 26:
Thinking About Decisions (page 74)

Session 27:
Decision Making Using the Five-Step Model (page 76)
Topic: Decision Making

We make decisions every day, from what we will eat to what we will do with our free time. These decisions are not difficult – we make them as a matter of course and give little thought to them. All decisions are not so simple, however. The two sessions in this section help peers to first look at how they make decisions and then to provide them with a five-part model that is useful when making decisions, or helping another to make a decision that will have both short- and long-term effects.

Advisor's Notes – Decision Making Using the Five-Step Model

Ice Breaker:
Stand back and notice who becomes leader, what decisions are made, how long the untangling takes, what sort of questions are asked, and so on. This activity can also be done non-verbally. In this case, you can either appoint a leader or let a leader emerge from the group. This ice breaker is an excellent learning activity for all.

Helping Skills Summary

The effective peer helper must be aware of these components when working with clients:

1. **Display** strong attending behavior – really listen to what the client has to say.

2. **Accept** the client's feelings – you need to respond with empathy.

3. **Establish** a welcoming environment where the client is encouraged to talk with the use of:

   - open questions,
   - open invitations to talk – "Tell me about... ," nodding your head and so on,
   - minimal encouragers that help the client to expand his or her story or elaborate on feelings – "Tell me more... ."

4. **Avoid** communication blockers – you need to be on guard for blockers that will stop effective communication.

5. **Paraphrase** – provide the client with feedback of the discussion to clarify for both parties – the client and you – what has been said.

6. **Reflect** feelings – give the client feedback on the emotions she or he has expressed – "You seem angry... pleased... sad... ."

7. **Summarize** – present a summary of the content and feelings the client has expressed during the meeting.

8. **Apply** the five-step decision making model – help the client apply the model to his or her problem.

Thinking About Decisions

Thinking about buying a new jacket? Perhaps you should complete this session and then decide.

Objectives:

▼ to think about the decisions you make on a daily basis,

▼ to think about how you make decisions,

▼ to appreciate that some decisions have greater consequences than others.

Ice Breaker:

Two Truths and a Lie

1. Think of two things about yourself that are true and which you will tell the rest of the group, for example, "I won the most valuable player award" and "I have a younger sister."

2. Now, think of a lie about yourself that you will tell the group.

3. As a group, elect a fellow peer member to be "It."

4. Form a large circle. One by one, each person tells one thing about himself or herself. If "It" thinks that what was said is the truth, she or he says, "It is good to tell the truth" and approaches someone else. If "It" feels that the peer has told a lie, "It" tells the peer, "It is a bad idea to tell a lie." If "It" was correct in guessing it was a lie, that peer must take over being "It."

(*Note:* "It" can approach anyone in the circle, that is, she or he does not have to move around the circle in sequence. Sometimes it is a good tactic to approach someone unexpectedly so she or he won't have time to prepare a lie.)

Activities:

1. Complete the chart on the next page.

2. Review your answers and come to a conclusion about how carefully you make decisions.

3. Respond to the following points in the spaces provided.

(a) Three routine decisions you make every day.

_____

_____

_____

(b) Importance of these decisions in your future.

_____

_____

_____

(c) Two decisions that a parent, teacher, pre-schooler, senior citizen, and volleyball coach will make today.

_____

_____

(d) Three people whom you believe make important decisions on a regular basis.

_____

_____

_____

(e) Some people have a secret when making a decision. If you agree with this statement, describe what you think is their secret.

_____

_____

_____

Discussion:

1. In small groups, make up a list of decisions that have to be made by a group in your school each day. You may want to target one group, for example, the office staff, the caretaking staff, or the student council.

2. Classify the decisions the group must make from simplest to most complex. How does the group arrive at making decisions? Is there a key decision-maker, or are decisions arrived at by group consensus?

Closure:

Record in your journal a major decision that you have made in your life during the past year.

Thinking About Decisions

When I make decisions about...	I think it through carefully	I give it some thought	I don't really think about it
Getting a haircut			
Choosing clothes to wear each day			
Completing homework			
Watching television			
Getting a part-time job			
Spending small amounts of money $5.00 or less			
Spending between $25.00 and $100.00			
Spending a large amount to buy a major purchase.			
Choosing courses at school			
Joining clubs, teams, or other activities			
Choosing a career			
Getting along with my family			
Planning ahead for my future			
Planning my weekend			

Decision Making Using the Five-Step Model

It is not hard to see that there is a difference between the simple (automatic) decisions that require little thought and energy, and the more complicated (major) decisions that require thought, time, and effort. This session takes you through the five-step decision-making model which you can use to make major decisions in your life, and in your work with fellow students.

Objective:

▼ to practise using the five-step decision-making model.

Ice Breaker:

A Huge Human Knot

1. Form a large circle.

2. Join your right hand with someone standing across from you in the circle.

3. When everyone has joined their right hand, join your left hand with another person anywhere in the circle.

4. The objective of the activity is to untangle this human "knot" while still holding hands.

Activity:

When a client asks you to help him or her solve a problem, you need to take the client through the five steps of decision making.

1. Help your client identify the problem by turning it into a question: "What should you do about... ?"

2. Together, explore the problem by brainstorming for alternatives, deciding on criteria, considering the consequences, and referring to the client's personal value system:

"What do you think you could do about this situation...?"

3. Help the client choose the best alternative.

4. Encourage the client to act on his or her choice. This is the time for the client to put the chosen alternative into operation:

"When will you do it? When would you like to meet again to discuss how things are going?"

5. Evaluate the results:

"How did it go? What would you do differently?"

Read the following problems. Choose one and apply the five-step decision-making model:

- You have to make a major decision regarding course selections for your future career.
- You have just seen someone cheating on an exam.
- Your friends have all started to drink. You feel embarrassed and are afraid they won't like you when you refuse to drink with them.

Discussion:

1. In small groups, discuss your reactions to this model. Did you find it easy to use? Why? Why not?

2. What would you do if you felt that you had helped a client make a wrong decision? Discuss your responses to this dilemma in your group.

Closure:

Complete the following sentence in your journal:

"If a client or a friend asks me to make a decision for him or her, I will..."

> ## A Five-Step Decision-Making Process
>
> ❶ **Identify** the central issue or problem.
>
> ❷ **Explore** the issue or problem and the alternatives and consequences.
>
> ❸ **Choose** a next step.
>
> ❹ **Act** upon your choice.
>
> ❺ **Evaluate** the results.

9

Practical Issues: Student Services

Introduction

Getting to know the people and the resources in the guidance office/student services department is a good idea for peer helpers, both professionally and personally.

Once the peer helpers know where to locate the information needed for career, educational, or referral purposes, they will be able to assist fellow students, friends, parents, or teachers in locating materials. Peers will be able to use the research knowledge they learned in training sessions to efficiently sort through the multitude of information found in the guidance office.

Peer helpers will have the advantage of being one of the first people to see the publications and updates as they come in to the guidance office. They will also be able to access various career/educational computer programs for their own benefit, as well as to instruct and guide others through such programs.

Helpful Hints to Facilitate these Exercises

1. Once the peer helpers have completed these worksheets, they can keep them in their journal for handy reference.

2. These exercises can be assigned as homework and done on the peer helper's own time. The sheets should be checked by you for accuracy of research technique and presentation of correct information.

3. Peers can also work with a partner or in triads to complete the exercises. This strategy works well since discussion is a natural outgrowth of pair and small-group work.

4. There are no ice breakers given for these exercises. Their aim is quite self-explanatory, and peers should have no difficulty in recognizing the intent of the activity.

Student Services Scavenger Hunt

Objectives:

▼ to develop an overview of guidance office resources,
▼ to know the names of the guidance/student services/school administration staff.

Activity:

Using the resources available in the guidance office, locate the following information. Please return all resources after you have used them.

1. Name three colleges that have a business accounting program. Give their location and length of course.

(a) _____

_____

(b) _____

_____

(c) _____

_____

2. List the high school courses needed to get in to the program in Question #1.

_____ _____

_____ _____

_____ _____

3. Where would you find occupational information on chemical engineering?

_____

4. List six universities in your province or state.

_____

_____

_____

_____

5. List two universities in your province or state that offer a program in kinesiology. Give the admission requirements for each program.

(a) _____

_____

(b) _____

_____

6. Find the median starting salary of early childhood education graduates in your province or state one year ago, the number of graduates working in the field today, and the total number of graduates.

_____ _____ _____

7. Where would you find post-secondary information?

_____

_____

8. Where would you find career information?

_____

_____

9. Where would you find information on government-sponsored programs?

_____

_____

10. A student inquires about post-secondary scholarships. Where would you direct him or her?

_____

_____

11. Name two alternatives for a high school graduate other than work, college, or university.

_____

_____

12. Name two careers a person who likes science might pursue.

_____

_____

13. Name two excellent post-secondary research books.

_____

_____

14. List the career, interest, or educational research programs we have available on the guidance office computer.

_____ _____ _____

_____ _____ _____

15. Name the following resource or support staff we call on for help.

Health nurse: _____

School social worker: _____

Board or district psychologist: _____

Others _____

_____

16. Name all guidance counsellors.

_____ _____

_____ _____

_____ _____

17. Name the principal's secretary.

_____

18. Name our school administration.

Principal _____

Vice-principal _____

Vice-principal _____

Now, get their autograph. Introduce yourself and have a brief talk with each person.

The Roles of Guidance/Student Services at Our School

Objectives:

▼ to become familiar with the role of the guidance counsellor, principal, vice-principal, and peer helpers,

▼ to know how guidance appointments are arranged and scheduled,

▼ to familiarize yourself with guidance office forms.

Activities:

1. Describe key responsibilities of:

(a) the guidance counsellor

_____

_____

_____

(b) the principal

_____

_____

_____

(c) the vice-principal

_____

_____

_____

(d) peer helpers

_____

_____

_____

2. How are guidance appointments scheduled?

_____

_____

_____

_____

3. A student may make a guidance appointment for these reasons:

_____   _____

_____   _____

4. A student may be referred to a guidance counsellor by any of the following people:

_____   _____

_____   _____

5. How does the department keep track of students who have used guidance services?

_____

_____

_____

6. What forms are used for:

referrals:

_____

daily progress reports:

_____

homework schedules:

_____

exam schedules:

_____

timetable changes:

_____

parental consent:

_____

class excusal:

_____

Timetable Know How

Objectives:

▼ to become familiar with making a timetable change,

▼ to become aware of factors to be considered when a student wants to make a timetable change.

Activity:

1. Look over the sample student timetable shown on the next page.

2. Answer the questions which follow the sample timetable. Refer to it when necessary.

Brad is a Grade 10 student taking courses on the semester system. Semester 1 runs from September until January; Semester 2 from February until June.

Use Brad's timetable to answer the following questions.

1. List the courses Brad is taking. Write their names in full.

Semester 1   Semester 2

_____   _____

_____   _____

_____   _____

_____   _____

2. At what level of achievement are most of his courses?

_____

3. At what grade level are most of his courses? _____

4. Why do you think he is taking physical education at the general level?

_____

5. Give reasons that would explain why Brad is enrolled in a first-year French course when he is in his second year of high school.

_____

_____

_____

6. How many credits are each of his courses worth?

_____

_____

7. What does "03" stand for at the end of MAT 2A1?

_____

8. Brad comes to you as a peer helper. He wants to drop BK 1 2G1. What questions might you ask him?

_____

_____

_____

_____

9. Brad is intent on dropping the course. What procedures do you follow?

_____

_____

_____

10. Brad now has a spare period, something which is only allowed at the senior level. He decides to take music, but it is not offered during the time he has available. Is this change possible?

_____

11. Who must you consult before you begin the corresponding paperwork?

_____

12. What other changes will have to be made to Brad's timetable?

_____

_____

_____

STUDENT SCHEDULE

COBOURG EAST COLLEGIATE

STUDENT: Dunlop, Bradley R.   GRADE: 10

HOME ROOM #:   242   HOMEROOM TEACHER: Ms.L. Warren

TIME	SEMESTER I	SEMESTER II
0:900 - 10:16	MAT 2A1 - 03 Mathematics Peters, Mr. Room 217	HCT 2A1 - 02 History Langford, Mrs. Room 102
10:16 - 11:32	PHM 2G1 - 02 Physical Education - Boys Knight, Mr. Gym "D"	BKI 2G1 - 01 Keyboarding Doyle, Mrs. Room 208
11:32 - 12:37	LUNCH	LUNCH
12:37 - 01:53	ENG 2A1 - 01 English Truelove, Mrs. Room 204	AVI 2A1 - 01 Visual Arts Brown, Mr. Room 121
01:53 - 03:09	FSF 1A1 - 03 French Biggs, Mme. Room 21	SNC 2A1 - 02 Science Passmore, Mr. Room 105

What Do You Know About Post-Secondary Education?

Objective:

♥ to assess your present knowledge concerning post-secondary education.

Activity:

Complete the following quiz by circling "T" for True and "F" for False. Check your answers at the end of the quiz.

1. **T F**   There is a minimum entrance requirement for colleges.

2. **T F**   There is a minimum entrance requirement for universities.

3. **T F**   Training to become a doctor, lawyer, or dentist is only available through universities.

4. **T F**   All post-secondary educational institutions offer on-site residences.

5. **T F**   All college courses have unlimited enrollment.

6. **T F**   Examples of limited enrollment programs at university are architecture, pharmacy, and physical and occupational therapy.

7. **T F**   College courses can vary anywhere from one through four years duration.

8. **T F**   Anyone who plans to attend a post-secondary educational institution can apply for a government loan.

9. **T F**   All professional programs take four or more years to complete.

10. **T F**   Apprenticeships are an excellent way to get an education because you get paid while learning on the job.

11. **T F**   Apprenticeships are easy to obtain.

12. **T F**   It is easy to enroll in the military.

13. **T F**   You need a four-year degree to enter the military.

14. **T F**   Colleges and universities offer co-operative programs.

Check your answers here:

1. T	6. T	11. F
2. T	7. F	12. F
3. T	8. T	13. F
4. F	9. T	14. T
5. F	10. T	

College and University Learning Package

Objective:

♦ to assist you in finding accurate information on two educational alternatives – colleges and universities.

Activity:

Use guidance office resources to answer the following questions:

1. There are _____ colleges in your province or state. Name three, and give their location and number of full-time students.

(a) _____

_____

(b) _____

_____

(c) _____

_____

2. When you finish college, you are granted a

_____

3. Provide a brief description of the following terms:
(a) technician

_____

(b) technologist

_____

(c) certificate program

_____

(d) upgrading

_____

(e) apprenticeship

_____

(f) continuing education

_____

4. An over-subscribed program is one where there are more applicants than there is room in the program; thus, they are also called limited enrollment programs. What criteria does a college consider for entrance to these programs?

_____

_____

_____

5. Post-secondary institutions charge a fee called tuition to attend their programs and classes. Circle the figure that most closely matches annual college tuition fees.

$300 $600 $1000 $1500 $2000 $3000 $6000

6. How much money would a student attending an out-of town college need in order to live, factoring in the cost of tuition, accommodation, books, transportation, and basic living expenses?

_____

_____

7. There are _____ universities in your province or state. Name three, and give their location and number of full-time students.

(a) _____

_____

(b) _____

_____

(c) _____

_____

8. Some universities are divided into campuses called colleges. Give one example.

_____

9. Upon graduation, university graduates receive a

_____ .

10. Provide a brief description of the following:

(a) BA

_____

(b) Hon BA

_____

(c) MA

_____

(d) B.Sc.

_____

(e) Ph.D.

_____

(f) Major

_____

(g) Minor

_____

(h) Undergraduate

_____

11. Post-secondary institutions charge a fee called tuition to attend their programs and classes. Circle the figure that most closely matches annual university tuition fees.

$300 $600 $1000 $1500 $2000 $3000 $6000

12. How much money would a student attending an out-of-town university need in order to live, factoring in the cost of tuition, accommodation, books, transportation, and basic living expenses?

_____

13. Student loans are available to help students pay for their education. What is the basis on which loans are granted?

_____

_____

14. Both colleges and universities offer bursaries. Describe a bursary, and what is required in order to receive one.

_____

_____

15. Some colleges and universities offer special programs. Briefly define the following:

(a) co-operative education

_____

_____

(b) work-study programs

_____

_____

(c) internship

_____

_____

(d) work experience

_____

_____

(e) job placement

_____

_____

Post-Secondary Alternative Learning Package

Objective:

▼ to learn about alternative post-secondary programs.

Activity:

1. List six post-secondary alternatives:

(a) _____

(b) _____

(c) _____

(d) _____

(e) _____

(f) _____

2. What is an apprenticeship?

_____

_____

3. Why do both employers and employees benefit from apprenticeships?

_____

_____

_____

4. As an apprentice, will your wage ever dip below the minimum wage required by law? _____

5. About _____ % of the apprenticeship program will be

spent at _____ .

The remainder of the program is usually spent at

_____ .

You may even be able to receive financial support from

the _____ .

6. The regulated and employer-established trades are grouped into four categories:

(a) _____

(b) _____

(c) _____

(d) _____

7. What is the minimal education requirement for most trades? _____
(Remember that additional education is perceived as an asset by almost all employers.)

8. How long are the following apprenticeships?

Each period is measured in _____ .

How many _____ would it take to become:

(a) a motor vehicle mechanic _____

(b) a tool and die maker _____

(c) an automotive painter _____

(d) a hairdresser _____

9. How do you become an apprentice?

_____

_____

10. Who would you contact to assess your academic and skill achievement? Could this same person help you draw up a contract between your employer and you, or would you need to approach another person?

_____

_____

11. Where is your closest apprenticeship branch office?

_____

12. Name two agricultural colleges and tell where each is located.

(a) _____

_____

(b) _____

_____

13. Identify which of the agricultural colleges offer the following programs:

(a) ornamental horticulture

_____

(b) equine technology

_____

(c) animal health technology

_____

(d) agriculture journalism

_____

14. What school would you attend to receive your Doctor of Chiropractic.

(a) _____

How long would it take to complete this program?

(b) _____

15. Research private vocational schools. Name one school that offers the following programs. Include the duration of the program.

(a) masseuse

_____

(b) locksmith

_____

(c) esthetician

_____

(d) private investigator

_____

(e) auctioneer

_____

Appendix

Advisor's Checklist

Let's look more closely at the things a peer helper advisor should consider before beginning to train peer helpers. These issues must be addressed before even initiating a peer helping program.

General Questions

What is the purpose or function of having a peer helping group in your school?

_____

_____

_____

What roles will the students perform?

_____

_____

_____

What role(s) will you perform?

_____

_____

_____

How much time can the students give to the program?

_____

How much time can you afford to offer to the program?

_____

_____

_____

Will anyone help you co-ordinate the peer helping program?

_____

_____

If you decide to begin a peer helping program, where will peer helpers meet and work? in a spare classroom? the library? a conference room? a resource room?

_____

Training

Do you feel confident enough and/or knowledgeable enough to do the training?

_____

How much time can you give to the actual training?

_____

How much time will it take to cover all the topics you feel are necessary?

_____

Can you call on the expertise of other professionals to help with the training?

_____

Are there other school staff to help you with the training?

_____

Where will special training sessions be held? at the school? at someone's house? in a retreat session?

_____

_____

Can students attend a weekend session or will the sessions have to be divided into smaller segments of time?

_____

_____

_____

Is it possible to run a conference where several schools or groups can be trained at the same time, making good use of many advisors and shared expertise?

_____

Session Format

Will you set objectives for each session?

_____

How will you incorporate the learning styles of the participants?

_____

_____

What will you include in each session, for example, ice breaker activity, new skill to be taught, demonstration, practice activities, processing and written work, follow-up activities?

_____

_____

_____

What topics do you think are important and necessary?

_____

_____

_____

What topics do other peer helping groups deem as very important?

_____

_____

What topics does your school administration want you to discuss?

_____

_____

_____

Program Size

How many students will be in your program?

_____

Will you train many students and then "cut" the peer helping group to a workable number after observing all the participants during the training sessions?

_____

_____

How long will you keep veteran peer helpers in the program? Will you accept a specified number of new candidates each year?

_____

_____

Do you want students from all the grades and all levels of study?

_____

Evaluation

Will you evaluate each training session or evaluate the total training?

_____

_____

_____

Do you have to justify your program and time spent on peer helping to anyone else?

_____

What was worthwhile about each activity? What needs to be improved?

_____

_____

_____

_____

_____

_____

_____

Peer Helper Application Form

Name: _____

Birthdate: _____

Address: _____

_____

_____

Phone: _____

Homeform: _____

Homeform Teacher: _____

1. Briefly describe what you believe are the personal qualities a peer helper should have.

_____

_____

2. Give examples of situations where you have shown these qualities.

_____

_____

_____

3. What do you like about the peer helper program?

_____

_____

_____

4. Why would you like to become a peer helper?

_____

_____

_____

5. List volunteer work and/or club activities in which you have been involved this year.

_____

_____

_____

6. Why is volunteering a good thing?

_____

_____

7. List activities or clubs you plan to join during the coming school year.

_____

_____

8. Would you be available for noon-hour meetings (approximately two per month)? Circle your answer:

Yes   **No**

9. What do you think are the greatest barriers to students accepting one another?

_____

_____

10. How would you handle these situations?
(a) You are Chairperson of our Christmas "Adopt-a-Family" campaign. You have asked a fellow peer helper to write announcements, but she has not done them.

_____

_____

_____

(b) You are having a stressful day and need to assess your commitments and priorities. Today, during lunch, the following activities are taking place. Prioritize these noon-hour events (1 being top priority):

____ sessional band practice

____ last-minute lunch date

____ peer helper meeting

____ intramural tournament

(c) While you are in the guidance office, you hear some "interesting" information about a student that you know other students would like to hear. You:

_____

_____

_____

11. As a peer helper, check when you are obligated to share a student's confidence with an adult counsellor or a teacher.

____ teen pregnancy   ____ time management

____ abuse   ____ failing grades

____ peer pressure   ____ vandalism

____ suicide   ____ alcohol abuse

12. List five things you would like to do as a peer helper.

(a) _____

_____

(b) _____

_____

(c) _____

_____

(d) _____

_____

(e) _____

_____

13. List your hobbies and interests.

_____   _____

_____   _____

_____   _____

_____   _____

14. How would you describe yourself, related to what you know about peer helping?

_____

_____

_____

_____

_____

_____

_____

_____

_____

_____

_____

_____

Interview Rating Chart

Sample Questions

1. What tasks should peer helpers perform in our school?

2. What activities will you be participating in next year?

3. What do you like best about yourself? Why do others like you?

4. What would you like to do when you finish high school?

5. What do high school students worry about?

6. If you were entrusted with a sensitive personal problem by a student, how would you handle it?

7. What approach would you take with a student who hates a teacher?

8. If you could change anything about the school, what would it be? Why?

9. (a) When you were in your first year of high school, what was your biggest worry?
(b) How could a peer helper have assisted you with this problem?

10. If a student is failing a subject, what would you recommend she or he do?

Additional Questions:

_____

_____

_____

_____

_____

_____

_____

Applicant: _____   **Interviewer:** _____

Part A (Application Form)

1. Time available/other commitments _____

2. Reasons for wanting to be a peer helper _____

3. Volunteer work/extra-curricular activities _____

Assessment   /30

Part B (Interview)

1. Ability to communicate _____

2. Enthusiasm _____

3. Sincerity _____

4. Reasons for wanting to be a peer helper _____

5. Time commitment _____

Assessment   /30

Rating Scale: 1 2 3 4 5 6 7 8 9 10

Low   High

❏ Accept   ❏ Waiting List

Sample Peer Helpers' Schedule

Month	Days	Particulars
August/September	Mon Aug 29– Fri Sep 2	Helping with tours, registration, timetables
September "Terry Fox" Run for Cancer Research United Way	Tues 6 Fri 9 Mon–Fri 12–16 Fri 16 begins	School begins – Assembly a) Welcome to the school for new students b) Visit Grade 9 homerooms Grade 9 Week First school dance
October "Kids Help Phone Line" United Way	Mon 10 Mon–Fri 17–21 Mon 17 Thurs 20 Fri 21 Mon–Fri 24–28 Thurs 27 Mon 31	Thanksgiving Day – no school AIDS Awareness Week University Information Program Bowl-a-thon for the "Kids Help Phone Line" P.A. Day Send-a-Treat Campaign Make treat bags Deliver treat bags to homerooms
November "Adopt-A-Family" begins	Wed–Fri 9–11 Fri 18 Mon 28	Provincial Peer Helpers Conference P.A. Day Toy-Food-Clothing drive begins ("Adopt-A-Family")
December Children's Wish Foundation "Adopt-A-Family"	Fri–Wed 9–21 Wed 14 Fri Dec 23–Fri Jan 6 Sat 31	Candy cane sales for "Children's Wish Foundation" Senior Citizens' Christmas Party Christmas Holidays First Night/New Year's Eve Celebration
January	Mon 9 Mon–Fri 9–13 Tues 10 Mon–Thurs 23–26 Fri 27–Tues 31	First Day Back Guidance Dept. visits feeder schools (Grade 8s) Grade 8 Parents' Night Exams!!! HOLIDAY TIME!! You deserve a break! "Changing Times...Changing Lives" Career Day for Grade 8s
February Heart & Stroke Foundation C.N.I.B.	Wed 1 Wed–Mon 1–6 Mon–Fri 20–24	P.A. Day Crocus plant sales for the Canadian National Institute for the Blind W.A.V.E. Week (We're Against Violence Everywhere)
March	Fri 10–17 Mon 20	March Break — HOLIDAY TIME!!! Daffodile pre-orders for Cancer Research
April Cancer Society	Fri 14–17 Mon–Fri 10–28	Easter Break Peer Helpers – recruitment and selection, executive selected
May Multiple Sclerosis	Wed–Fri 3–5 Fri 5 Mon–Tues 15–16 Fri 19 Mon 22	Peer Helpers Conference Carnation Sales for Multiple Sclerosis Society Student Leaders Workshop at Queen's University Grade 8 Day Victoria Day
June	Mon 5 Wed–Tues 21–27 Wed 28 Mon–Thurs 19–22	Write letters to Grade 8s Training Session and Peer Helper party on the last day of exams Commencement (ushers and guides) Exams!!! HAVE A SAFE & HAPPY SUMMER HOLIDAY!!!

Feelings Chart

Happy	Sad	Strong	Weak	Confused	Angry	Afraid
alive	alone	able	ashamed	anxious	aggravated	alarmed
amused	apathetic	accomplished	beaten	baffled	agitated	anxious
blissful	bothered	active	confused	bewildered	annoyed	apprehensive
bubbly	burdened	adequate	crazy	bothered	betrayed	chicken
calm	crushed	aggressive	defenceless	crazy	bitter	confused
cheerful	deflated	brave	doomed	depressed	bugged	cornered
comfortable	dejected	capable	exhausted	dismayed	burned up	desperate
content	depressed	competent	frail	distracted	cheated	distrustful
delighted	disappointed	eager	gentle	distraught	crabby	fearful
ecstatic	disenchanted	energetic	helpless	disturbed	disgusted	frightened
elated	distressed	firm	inadequate	doubtful	dissatisfied	harassed
enthralled	disturbed	forceful	inferior	embarrassed	disturbed	horrified
excited	down	important	insecure	flustered	enraged	insecure
exuberant	downhearted	open	lacking	forgetful	grouchy	intimidated
fantastic	dreary	positive	lethargic	frustrated	fed up	jumpy
fine	dull	powerful	lost	helpless	frustrated	lonely
fortunate	embarrassed	responsible	mild	hopeless	furious	meek
friendly	emotional	robust	passive	lost	hateful	nervous

Happy	Sad	Strong	Weak	Confused	Angry	Afraid
good	empty	safe	powerless	mistaken	hostile	overwhelmed
lively	gloomy	smart	shaken	misunderstood	hot-tempered	panic-stricken
merry	hurt	together	shattered	mixed up	impatient	panicky
marvellous	left out	trustful	submissive	muddled	intense	petrified
overjoyed	lonely	valuable	unsure	out-of-it	irate	pressured
peaceful	lost	vibrant	useless	puzzled	irritated	rattled
pleased	low	vigorous	weakened	surprised	livid	shaky
proud	miserable	zealous	worn out	trapped	mad	shy
relieved	moody			troubled	mean	stunned
satisfied	sorry			uncertain	outraged	tense
thankful	terrible			uncomfortable	perturbed	terrified
uplifted	unhappy			undecided	provoked	terrorized
wonderful	unloved			unsure	rage	threatened
	unpleasant			upset	revengeful	timid
	unwanted			vague	seething	tormented
	upset			weak	spiteful	uneasy
					stormy	unpleasant
					temper	unsure
					troubled	worried

95

Bibliography

Axford, M. *Me 'N You: Go Hug that Kid*. Toronto, Ontario: Lugus Publications, 1993.

Bach, Dr. G., & Dr. H. Goldberg. Creative *Aggression: The Art of Assertive Living*. New York, New York: Doubleday, 1974.

Billing D. *Starting a Peer Helping Program*. Picton, Ontario: Booklet produced for and by the Ontario Peer Helpers' Association, 1987.

Carr, R., & G. Saunders. Peer *Counselling Starter Kit*. Victoria, British Columbia: Peer Resources, 1979.

Faber, A., & E. Mazlish. *How to Talk So Kids Will Listen and Listen So Kids Will Talk*. New York, New York: Avon Books, 1980.

Fensterheim, H., Ph.D. & J. Baer. *Don't Say Yes When You Want to Say No*. New York, New York: Dell, 1975.

Harris, B.C. *Self-Awareness Workbook*. Toronto, Ontario: University of Toronto Guidance Centre, 1982.

Loraine, T. *Let Me Help You*. Computer software program. Toronto, Ontario, 1985.

Malik, C. *Positive Life-Using Skills: An Intermediate Prevention Programme*. Scarborough, Ontario: Alcohol and Drug Commission, 1985.

Myrick, R., & T. Erney. *Caring and Sharing: Becoming a Peer Facilitator*. Minneapolis, Minnesota: Educational Media Corporation, 1978.

Myrick, R.D., & T. Erney, *Youth Helping Youth: A Handbook for Training Peer Facilitators*. Minneapolis, Minnesota: Educational Media Corporation, 1979.

Peavy, R.B. *Adults Helping Adults: An Existential Approach to Co-operative Counselling*. Victoria, British Columbia: University of Victoria, 1978.

Smith, M. J., Ph.D. *When I Say No I Feel Guilty*. New York, New York: Dial Press, 1975.

Tindall, J.A., & H.D. Gray. Peer *Power: Becoming an Effective Peer Helper*. Muncie, Indiana: Accelerated Development, Inc., 1985.